A Visual Geography of Ghana

S. Asamoah Darko
M.A., Ph.D.
Senior Lecturer in Geography, University of
Science and Technology, Kumasi

Evans

Evans Brothers Limited

Published by Evans Brothers Limited
Montague House, Russell Square
London WC1B 5BX

Evans Brothers (Nigeria Publishers) Limited
PMB 5164, Jericho Road
Ibadan

First published 1973
Second impression 1974

Illustrations and maps by Leslie S. Haywood

Note for the pupils
Important geographical terms have been
printed in italics to bring them to your
notice. Where the meanings of any words
remain in doubt, ask your teacher to
explain them to you.

Metric equivalents for all measurements
have been given in the text and on maps.

Acknowledgements

The publishers are grateful to the following for
permission to reproduce the photographs which
illustrate this book:

Barnaby's Picture Library: pages 35, 56 (top right)
Cadbury Schweppes Limited: page 21 (top right)
J. Allan Cash: pages 13, 15 (bottom), 16, 19 (left),
25 (right), 32 (top), 34 (right), 41 (bottom left and
right), 44 (bottom), 45 (bottom right), 47, 56
(bottom left and right), 58
Commonwealth Institute: pages 19 (right), 45
(bottom left), 46 (bottom left and right)
Conway Picture Library: pages 18, 22 (bottom left),
36 (top right), 51
John Douglas: pages 9 (bottom), 26 (bottom left),
44 (top right), 46 (top left), 57, 61 (bottom right)
Ghana Academy of Sciences: page 27 (top)
Ghana Information Services: pages 14, 15 (top),
17, 20 (bottom), 24 (left), 26 (top and bottom right),
28 (top), 36 (bottom), 37 (bottom), 38 (top right),
40 (bottom left), 42 (middle left and bottom), 53
(bottom right), 60, 61 (top)
Miss Vera Johnston: page 23 (left)
Douglas Pike: page 33 (bottom right), 34 (left),
41 (top left)
Popperfoto: pages 6, 7, 8, 20 (top), 21 (top left),
22 (top right), 25 (left), 27 (bottom), 28 (bottom),
29, 30, 31, 32 (bottom), 33 (top), 37 (top), 38
(bottom), 45 (top left), 56 (top left), 59 (left)
P. B. Redmayne: page 38 (top left)
B. W. Smith Limited: pages 40 (bottom right),
41 (top right), 45 (top right), 54, 55, 59 (right)
Volta Aluminium Company Limited: pages 9 (top),
39, 40 (top left), 42 (top right), 49
W. D. & H. O. Wills: page 24 (right)

Printed by Tinling (1973) Limited, Prescot Lancs. (a member of the Oxley Printing Group Ltd.)
ISBN   0   237   28517   7   PRA   3984

Contents

1. Ghana in a World Setting

Ghana is one of the smallest countries in that part of the African continent which is called Tropical Africa, between latitude $23\frac{1}{2}°$ North and $23\frac{1}{2}°$ South. (See the map of the world below.)

Latitude is distance from the equator measured in degrees. The equator is latitude 0°, the North Pole is 90° North, the South Pole is 90° South. What is the latitude of Accra?

Tropical areas include the warmest parts of the earth's surface. There are also tropical areas in the Americas, in Asia, in Australia and in Oceania, the islands of the Pacific Ocean. The temperatures of tropical areas are not always or everywhere the same; for example, winds from the oceans or from neighbouring large areas of land and the height of the land above sea level can all affect the temperature.

The height of land above sea level is called *relief*. A *relief map* is a map which shows the different heights of land in a country.

Another continent, South America, is like Africa in one way. A large part of its land mass lies across and on each side of the equator.

Because it lies in the *tropics*, as the tropical areas are often called, Ghana supplies a number of tropical products to temperate lands where the climate is too cool for such crops to grow. *Temperate* lands are lands where it is seldom very hot or very cold. In return, Ghana buys such products as wheat from temperate countries.

The distance from Accra to London is almost 3,000 miles (4,800 km). A fast aircraft, such as the VC10, travelling without stopping, takes about six hours for this journey. A passenger ship sailing to Liverpool from Tema, the deep-water port near Accra, takes 12 days. People travelling from West Africa to the United Kingdom nearly always disembark (go ashore) at the main port of Liverpool. Accra is also a long way from other great cities such as

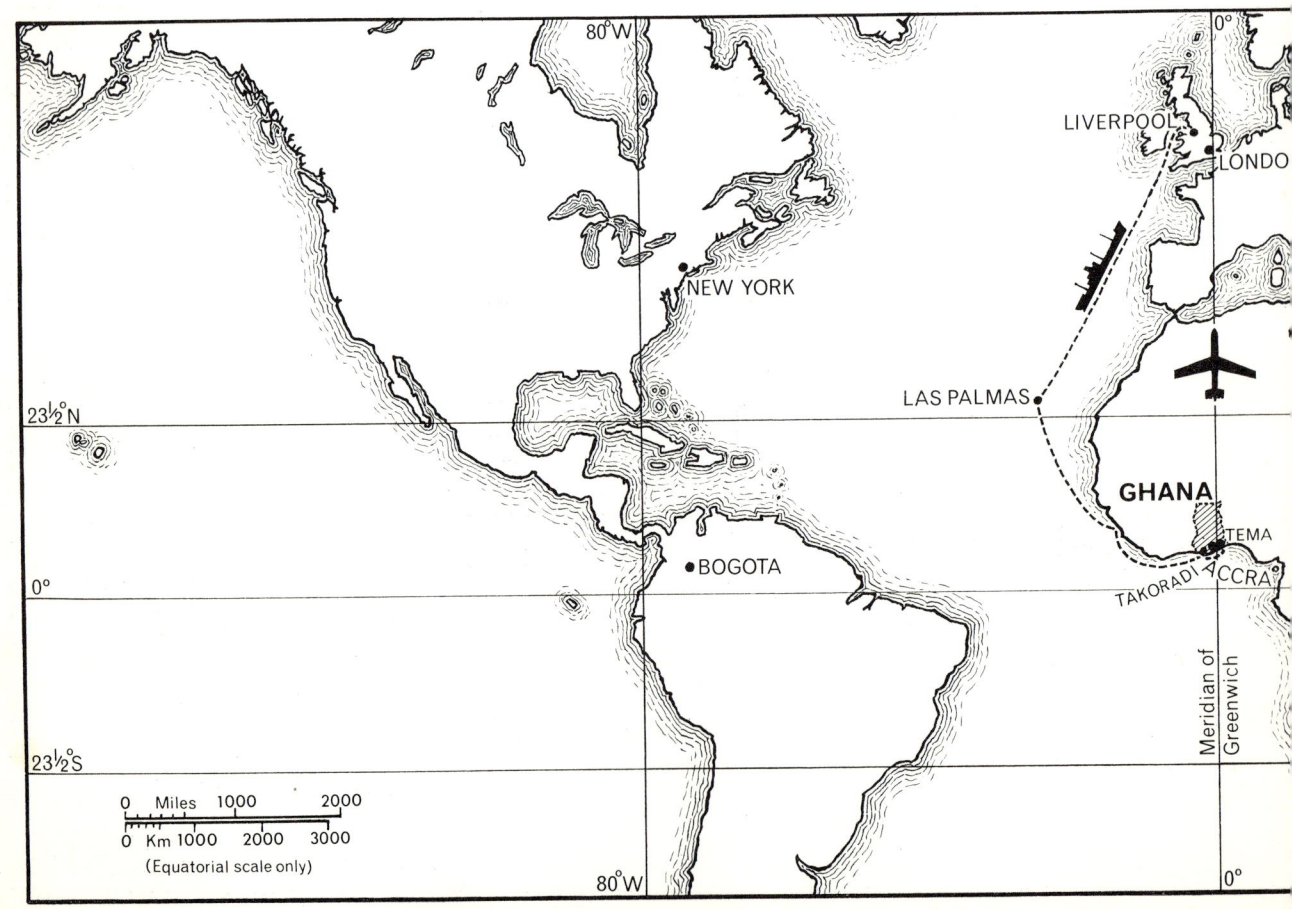

2

London, New York, Buenos Aires, Moscow, New Delhi, Djakarta and Sydney.

Although Accra and London are far apart, they have the same time. When it is midday or noon in Accra, it is also midday in London. This is because they are on the same longitude, the meridian of Greenwich.

A *meridian* is an imaginary circle running round the earth, passing through any place (e.g. Accra) and through the North and South Poles. The *prime* (or first) *meridian* (longitude 0°) is imagined as running through *Greenwich*, in London, where the British Royal Observatory used to be. *Longitude* is distance east or west of the prime meridian, measured in degrees.

Accra and London have the same time because they are on the same longitude, but they have different temperatures because they are on different latitudes. London lies on latitude 51° 30′ North. This shows that it is in the temperate region and so it is much cooler than Accra. The greater distance a place lies from the equator, the lower generally is its temperature.

On the map you can see that Accra is almost on the same latitude as Colombo in Ceylon, so that they have the same kind of temperature. But they are separated by 80 degrees of longitude and so they do not have the same time. The sun has its noon (when it is directly overhead) in Colombo 3½ hours before it has its noon in Accra. On the other hand, Accra time is three hours ahead of that in Bogota in Columbia (South America).

Exercises

1. Use a map to find out how many times the U.S.A. is bigger than Ghana.
2. Explain why tropical lands are warmer than those in the temperate regions.
3. Make a list of Ghana's tropical products.

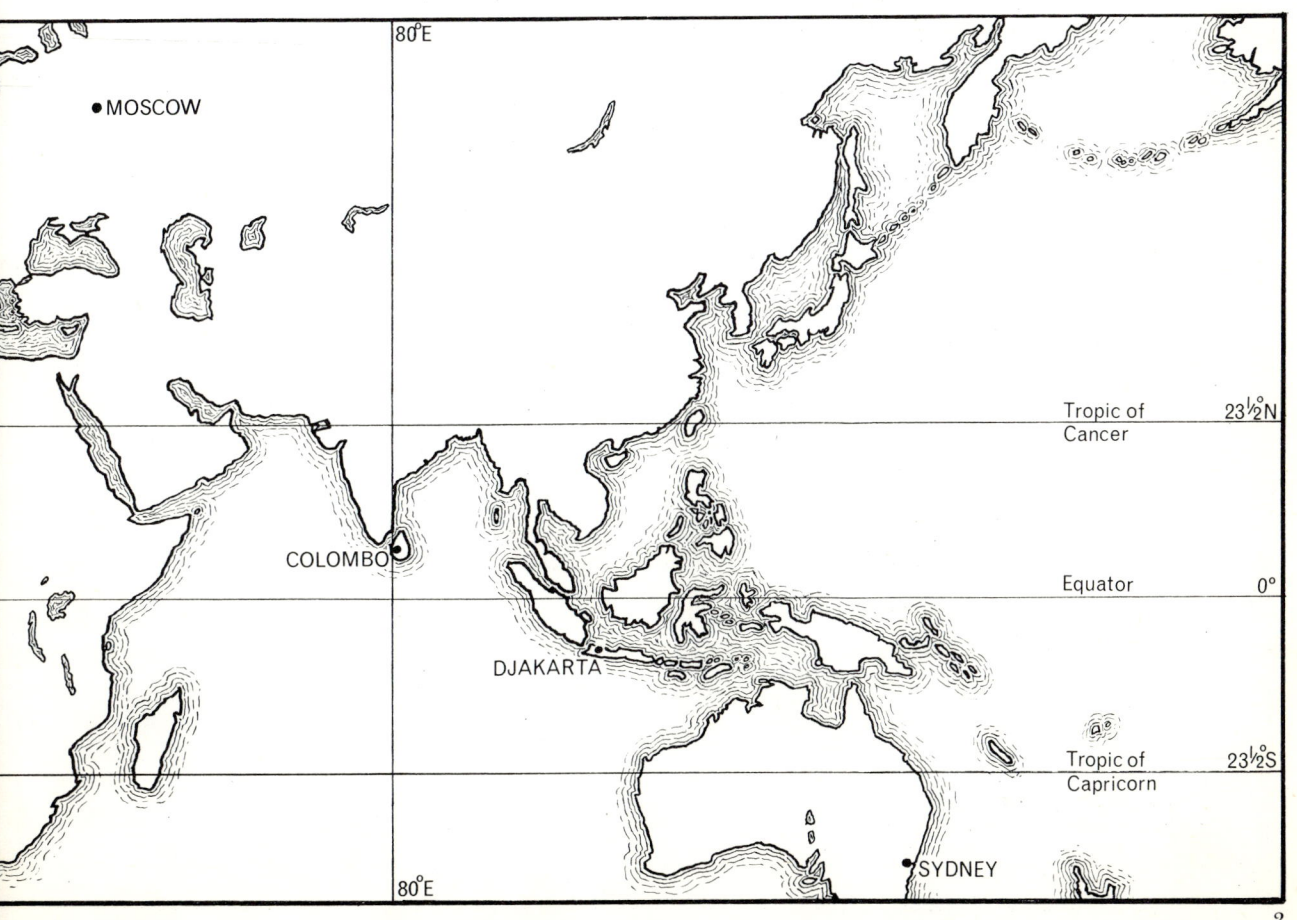

2. Ghana and its Neighbours

In Chapter 1 we said that Ghana was a small tropical country. It has an *area* of about 92,000 square miles (230,000 sq. km) and a *population* of 8½ million people. Ghana, which used to be called the Gold Coast, was one of four British West African countries, all of which are now independent. The other three are Nigeria, Sierra Leone and The Gambia. From the map below you can see that Ghana is smaller than Nigeria but bigger than Sierra Leone or The Gambia. The four countries are separated, and almost surrounded, by former French West African countries. (See the map below.)

Ghana was the first of the four countries to gain its independence from the United Kingdom. This happened on 6 March 1957 when Ghana took its present name. Like the other three countries it is a full and independent member of the Commonwealth and still has strong ties with the United Kingdom. Because of their connection with the United Kingdom the four countries are alike in some ways. For example, they use similar systems of money, they have the same official language (English) and their educational systems are similar.

On a map, Ghana has an oblong shape. It has the Gulf of Guinea on its southern *boundary*, or edge, the Ivory Coast in the west, Upper Volta in the north and Togo to the east. These three countries are Ghana's immediate neighbours. Ghana is separated from these immediate neighbours by boundaries which were drawn by Britain, France and Germany. Some of these international boundaries divide ethnic groups. For example, boundaries divide some of the Ewe, in south-east Ghana, from the rest of the group. Boundaries also divide the Angi in west Ghana and the Lobi and the Sisila in north Ghana. For this reason they are not satisfactory.

Other neighbours, not so close physically or in their way of life to Ghana, are Liberia, Guinea, Mali, Niger and Dahomey. Ghana once formed a union with Guinea and Mali which now no longer exists. All independent African states, however, are members of the Organization of African Unity.

Ghana tries to be close friends with all her neighbours. Some of the people of other West African countries live and work in Ghana. Ghanaians also go to other countries.

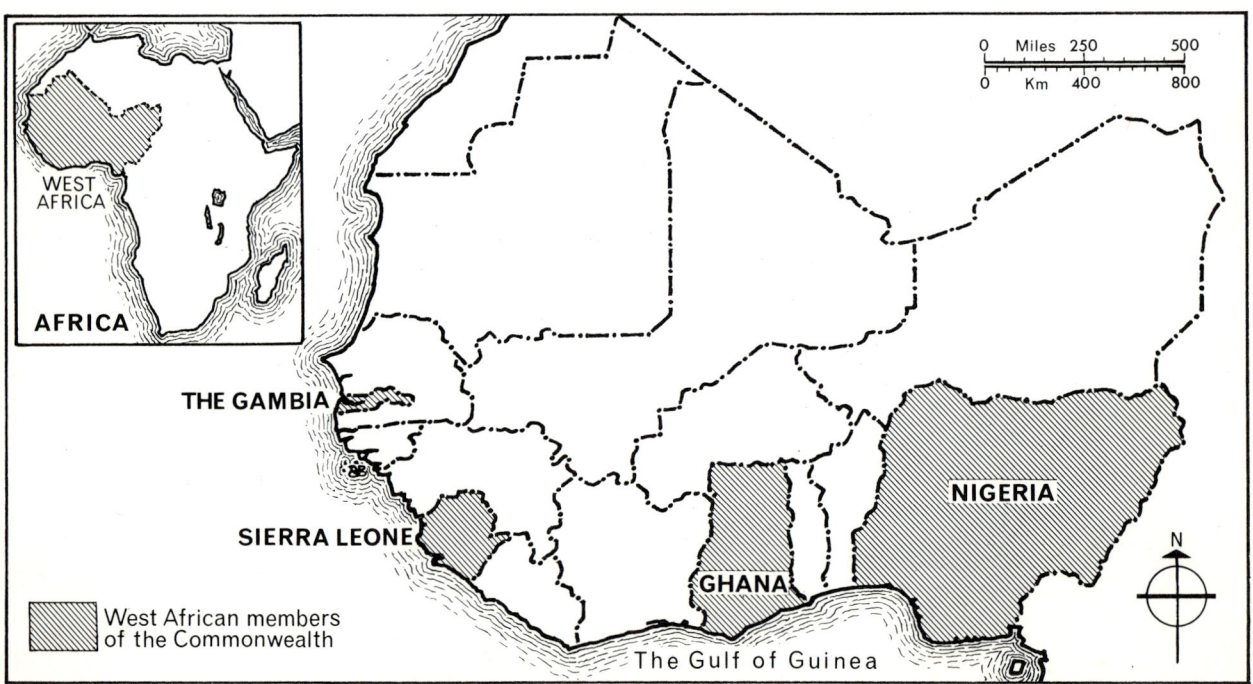

WEST AFRICA

AFRICA

THE GAMBIA

SIERRA LEONE

GHANA

NIGERIA

West African members of the Commonwealth

The Gulf of Guinea

N

As you would expect, Ghana and its neighbours have the same kind of problems—problems of earning a living (economic problems), of living together as a community (social problems), of overcoming difficulties of nature (physical problems)—and so they try to co-operate in trade, commerce (business), education and research. Representatives from Ghana and the neighbouring countries often meet to talk about trade, agriculture, health, education and sport.

Exercises
1. When was the Organization of African Unity (OAU) formed? Name its headquarters.
2. Locate on a map the ethnic groups whose lands are crossed by international boundaries. Show also the groups which are divided by international boundaries.
3. Trace the map on page 4. Write the names of the capitals of all countries in West Africa in the correct places on the map.
4. When did Ghana gain its independence?

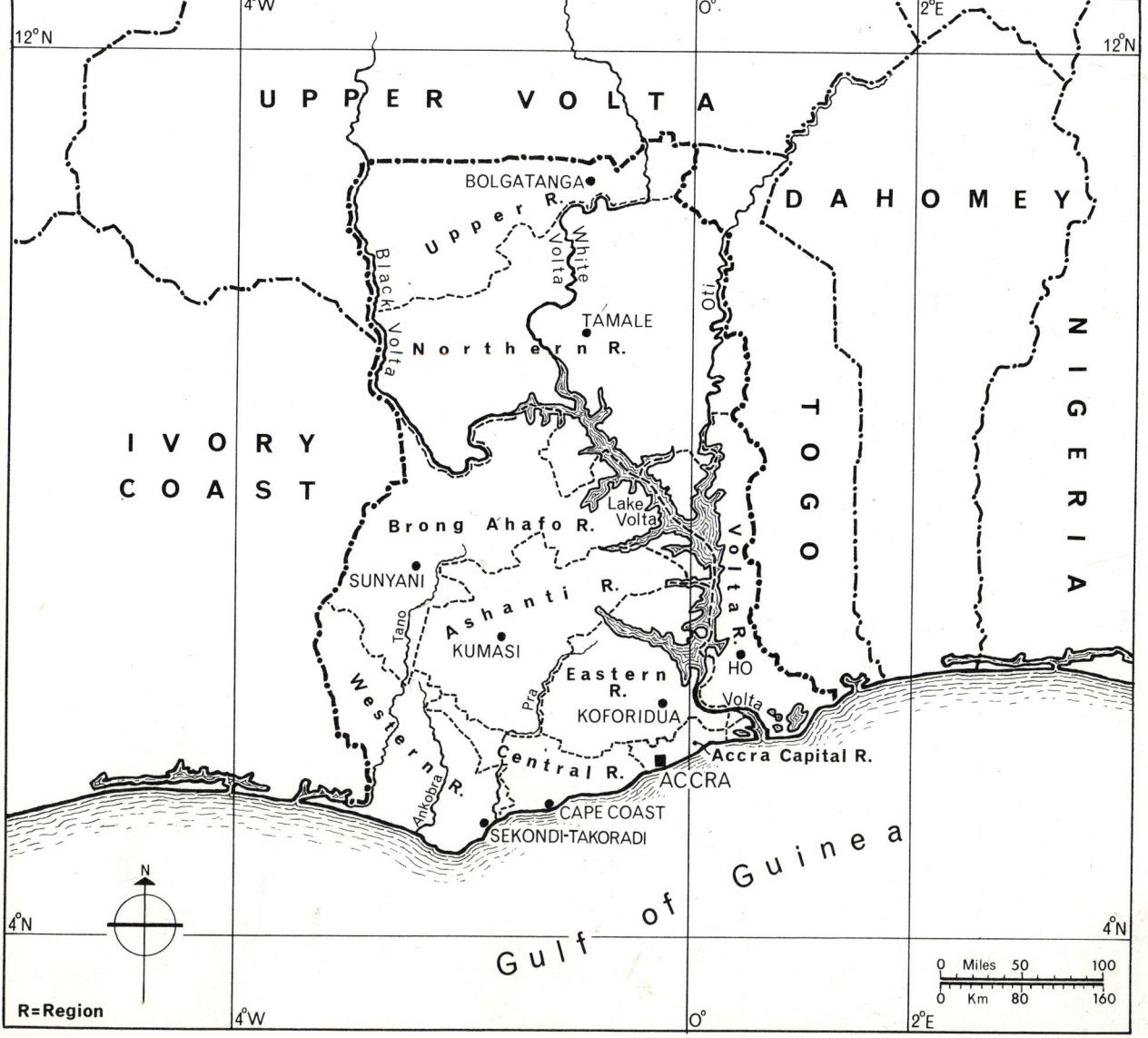

Ghana

3.   The Regions and Peoples of Ghana

Before 1900 the regions of South Ghana, Ashanti/Brong Ahafo, North Ghana and the Volta Region were separate. Today Ghana is one country. Let us look at how the country's compact area of about 92,000 square miles (230,000 sq. km) has been built up, and also look at the main ethnic groups of Ghana.

How Ghana was built up

The first European traders to come to the shores of Ghana were the Portuguese in 1481. They traded in gold and built a fort, Elmina Castle, in 1482. They were followed by the Dutch (people from the Netherlands), who traded in slaves and built forts at Mouri and Butri in 1624 and 1640. Other European traders who later came to the coast of Ghana were the Swedes, the French, the Germans, the Danes (people from Denmark) and the English. Most of them built castles along the coast, in which they kept slaves and stored goods for trade.

By 1850 almost all of them had gone, except the British who were left alone in control of the coastal strip of what is now Ghana. Earlier, in 1844, the British had signed a treaty with the Fanti people (known as the Bond of 1844), which gave them a little control over the Fanti.

The British conquered the Ashanti people in 1874, and signed treaties of friendship with many north Ghanaian chiefs in the last decade of the nineteenth century. However, it was not until January 1902 that these areas were declared as parts of Ghana. Before that date Ashanti/Brong Ahafo and North Ghana were independent of the British.

A large part of the Volta Region and the eastern side of North Ghana were sections of a German territory, known as Togoland. Germany lost Togoland after the First World War (1914–18). It was divided into two; one part went to Britain and the other to France. The two halves of Togoland were known as 'trust territories', because Britain and France held them on behalf of the League of Nations, a union of countries formed after the First World War to promote peace among nations. In 1950 the 'trust territory' of Togoland which was held by the British became part of Ghana.

At Independence in 1957, the regions of Ghana and their capitals were:

region	capital
East	Koforidua
West	Cape Coast
Ashanti/Brong Ahafo	Kumasi
North	Tamale
Volta	Ho

An early print of the Danish fort at Christiansborg

Both the European forts and the division of the country into regions have had some important effects. Many of the towns along the coast developed around European forts. This was because the people who lived on the coast were interested in trade. Also some of the coastal forts and castles offered them protection against their enemies.

The division of Ghana into regions has made the management of the country much easier. At the same time it has helped towards the growth of towns. The principal towns of Ghana are mostly national or regional centres and have large populations. Sunyani and Bolgatanga have been developing rapidly as towns since they were made regional centres. The regions also compete with each other in such activities as sports and school awards.

The main ethnic groups of Ghana

Ghanaians belong to different ethnic groups. People of a group often have the same *dialect* (their local language) and customs. These make them feel united. There are many ethnic groups in Ghana: some of the principal ones are Ashanti, Fanti, Ga, Adangme, Ewe, Guan, Buem, Mamprusi, Gonja, Dagomba, Krachi, Lawra, Tumu, Wala and Nanumba.

The love of their ethnic group can encourage people to take a keen interest in self-help work, for example building schools and road-making. But love of an ethnic group should not make us forget that the group is safe only in a strong, prosperous and united country. Our first loyalty, therefore, is to our country, the nation of Ghana.

Since Independence, the number of regions has been increased to nine. Some use the former names and others use new names. The nine regions are:

region	capital
Accra-Tema	Accra
Eastern	Koforidua
Central	Cape Coast
Western	Sekondi-Takoradi
Ashanti	Kumasi
Brong Ahafo	Sunyani
Northern	Tamale
Upper	Bolgatanga
Volta	Ho

Elmina Castle

Exercises

1. Draw a sketch map of Ghana, and mark on it the regions of the country and their capitals.
2. Find out from your history books six castles built along the coast of Ghana. Who built them and why were they constructed? Find on a map the towns in which they are situated.
3. Name your ethnic group and the other ethnic groups which surround it. Show how the ethnic groups you have listed are different.

7

4. The Relief of Ghana

The *relief* of a country means the different heights and kinds of landforms that are found there. The relief of Ghana is varied. There are sandbars, lagoons, plains, peneplains, plateaux, ridges, a crater and a big river basin. They are all explained below.

Sandbars are banks of sand that grow up at the mouth of a river or along a shore. *Lagoons* are usually shallow stretches of salt water, partly or completely separated from the sea by a strip of sand. *Plains* are large areas of land which is flat or nearly flat, generally low-lying. *Peneplains* are areas of land which are nearly plains, worn almost flat by wind and rain. *Plateaux* (or plateaus) are level areas high above sea level. *Ridges* are long, narrow areas of high land above the top of a line of hills. A *crater* is the mouth of a volcano (see page 15). A *river basin* is the whole area from which a river gathers its water.

This varied relief is caused by (i) differences in the kinds of rocks between one part of the country and another, (ii) the wearing-away of the rocks by wind and rain, heat and cold (this is called weathering or *erosion*), (iii) movements of the earth (known as *folding* and *faulting*) and (iv) volcanoes.

From the map opposite you can see that Ghana can be divided into four main relief regions:
(A) The coastal plains (B) The divided uplands and plateaux (C) The *scarps* (steep slopes) and ridges round the Volta basin (D) The Volta basin

The coastal plains (A) are very low-lying and are narrow in the east, broad in the west. On these plains, especially in the east, there are steep-sided, isolated hills known as *inselbergs* (from two German words meaning 'island mountains'). They are made of rocks which are so hard that weathering and erosion have not been able to wear them away to the level of the surrounding plains.

The divided uplands and plateaux (B) cover a much larger area. Their height is between 500 and 1,000 feet (150–300 metres). On these plateaux are a number of mountain ranges, such as Atewa-Atewiredu, Aboabo-Obuom and Dompim.

Around the Volta basin, marked on the map, are the Akwapim-Togo Hills, the Koforidua-Wenchi scarp, the northward-running plateaux in the west

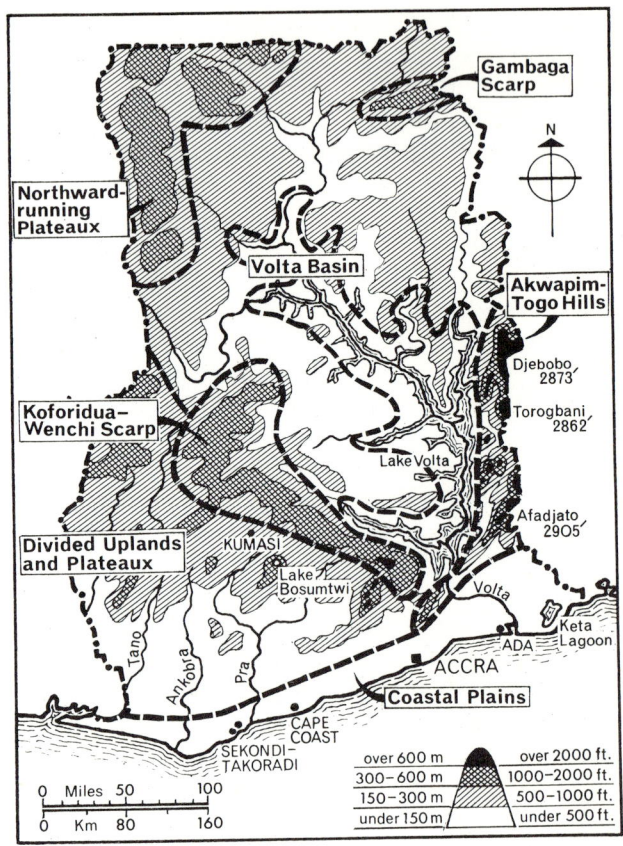

A relief map of Ghana

The hills at Amedzofe

The Volta basin

An inselberg on the Accra plains

and the Gambaga scarp (C). A scarp is the steep side of a hill. In the extreme north-east of the Togo hills is the highest point in Ghana. Most of these hills are *watersheds* (high land from which rivers flow) and many of them have *forest reserves* (land kept only for growing trees and not used for farming or building houses). There are few roads and farming is difficult. When the population grows and needs more food, the land will have to be farmed. The trees help to hold the soil together with their roots and the dead leaves feed the soil, so that it will become good land for farming in the future.

The Volta basin (D) was made by the sinking of the land very long ago. It is very large and wide. In the centre is Lake Volta about which we shall have much to say later. The surrounding ridges and plateaux make the basin look like a saucer. On each side of the river there are *terraces* or flat land which rises like steps. These show that either the land has risen or the sea level has fallen. Parts of the Volta basin are *flooded* or covered by water in the rainy season. This is partly because of the low level of the land so that the water cannot run away, and partly because in places there are layers of a kind of rock called *laterite* which prevents the water from sinking easily into the ground. These 'waterproof layers' are called *hardpans*.

Exercises

1. Draw a cross-section to show the shape of a scarp. (A cross-section is a drawing of what a solid object would look like if it was cut through. Look at the example on page 13.)
2. Draw a map of West Africa and show on it four watersheds.
3. Draw a line from (a) to (b) on the map and then draw a rough cross-section along this line to show the relief. Name on the cross-section the important kinds of relief along the line.

5. Weather and Climate

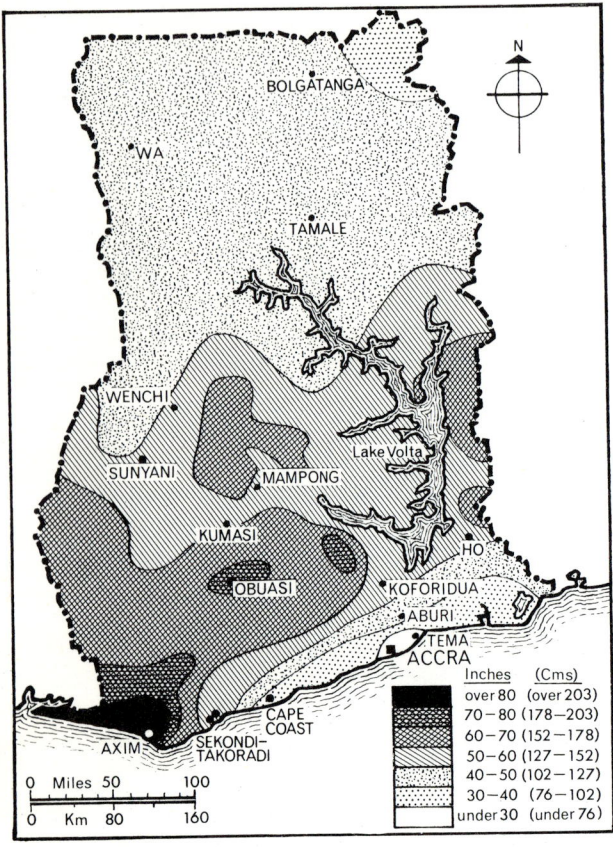

Rainfall distribution map

Inches (Cms)

■	over 80 (over 203)
	70–80 (178–203)
	60–70 (152–178)
	50–60 (127–152)
	40–50 (102–127)
	30–40 (76–102)
	under 30 (under 76)

The weather affects our everyday life. It is always changing. Today it may be bright and sunny, but tomorrow the weather may change. The sky may be dark with heavy clouds. Rain may fall and there may be thunder and lightning.

On radio and television, the 'weather man' tells us about the weather. He gives a short account of the weather in the last 24 hours and tells us what weather we can expect in the next 24 hours.

What are the things the weather man talks about? Sunshine, clouds, humidity, temperature, pressure, winds and rainfall. *Humidity* is the amount of moisture in the air. *Temperature* tells us how hot or cold it is. It is measured by a *thermometer*. *Pressure* is the force or 'weight' of the atmosphere. Pressure is measured by a *barometer*, winds by an *anemometer*, and rainfall by *a rain gauge*. Do you have a weather chart in your class? Tell your teacher about the weather of the last day recorded.

It is important to know something about the weather. Farmers must have some knowledge of the weather so that they know how to protect their crops. Pilots of aircraft must know about it too, so that they are prepared for the changes that may happen.

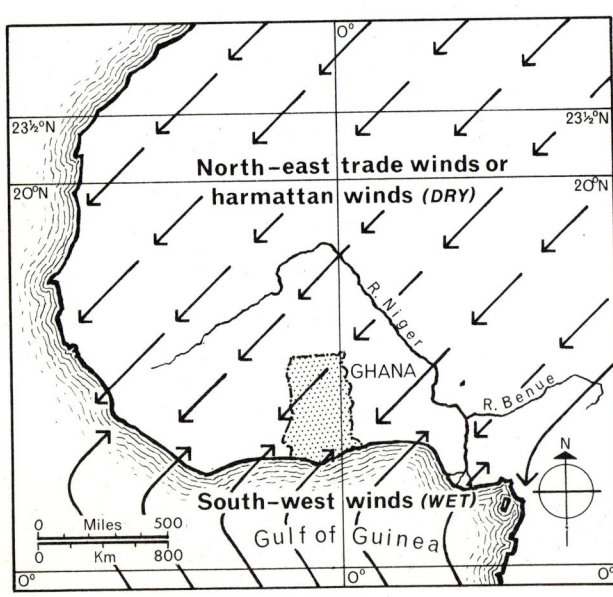

Main January winds

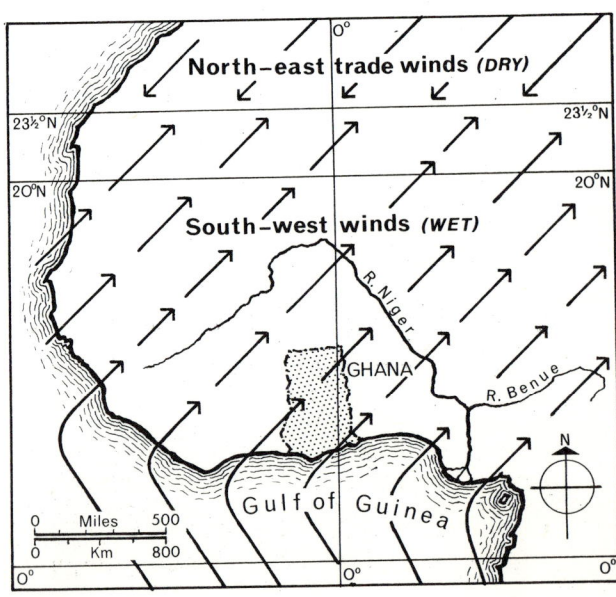

Main July winds

Climate is the average of the weather conditions studied over a long time—in the case of Ghana, about 35 years. The main elements of climate are the same as those of weather: temperature, pressure, winds and rainfall.

The sun is the main source of the earth's heat. Ghana is warm because it is in the tropics. Temperature is therefore not a serious problem for crops and people. In some countries the temperature is very low in winter; crops cannot grow properly there and men have to heat their rooms and wear thick clothes.

The element of climate which is most important in Ghana is rainfall. For this reason it is better to divide the year into rainy and dry seasons than into summer, autumn, winter and spring, which are the *seasons* for people in temperate areas.

The rainfall of Ghana is brought by winds which blow from the sea; these wet winds are known as '*south-westerlies*', because they blow from the south-west. These winds are largely seasonal but over the coastal areas they blow throughout the whole year. They begin to move northwards from February and reach their northernmost limit about July, when they begin to withdraw. In about September they are followed by the *harmattan* winds which are dry and come from the Sahara.

The two main causes of the rains in Ghana are:

(1) when the wet winds come to mountains in their way, they rise to cross them.

(2) when the winds pass over warm land they rise, because warm air always rises.

In both cases, the winds are forced to rise and as they rise they reach the cold air high above the ground and become cooler. (See the diagrams below.) *Vapour* is water carried in the air, like mist. When it cools, it becomes thicker and finally falls as rain. Rains which fall when they hit mountains are known as *relief rains*, and those which fall because of heating are called *convectional rains*. There is a third type, known as *frontal rains*. In Ghana these rains are very heavy and come with *squalls*, which are stormy winds. Squalls are the result of a meeting of south-west winds and wet winds from the east, which blow at great heights before they reach West Africa.

As you can see from the map on page 10, some parts of Ghana have more rain than others. The wet areas are either in the path of the rain-carrying winds or on high land. The south-east and the north do not have heavy rains. In the south-east the winds do not hit the coast because they blow along it and not directly inland. The north is far inland and the south-west winds reach there late and leave early.

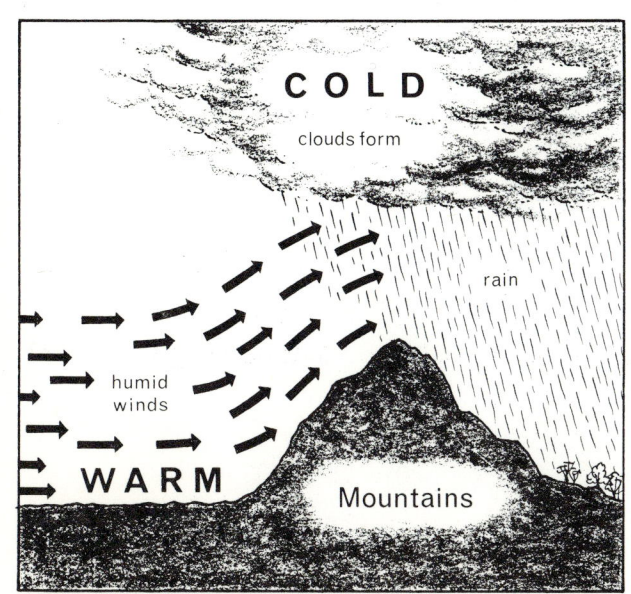

Relief rains

Convectional rains

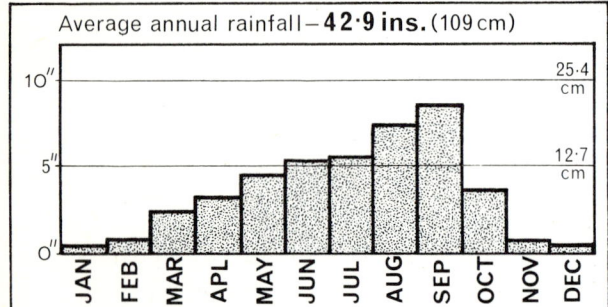

Tamale

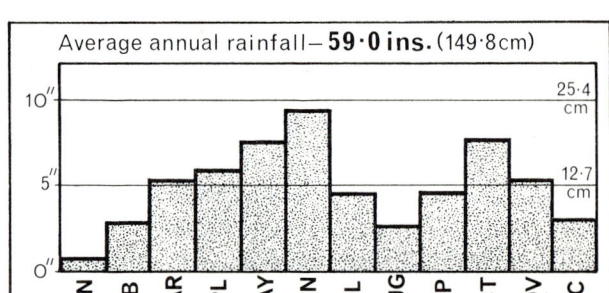

Wa

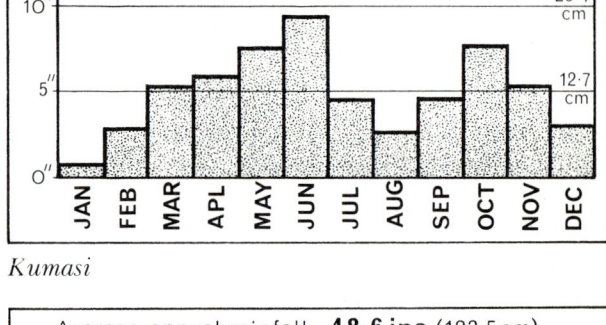

Kumasi

Look carefully at the graphs shown on this page and you will be able to tell your teacher how much rainfall there is in four different parts of Ghana throughout the year. You will see that towns in the north have one rainy season while those in the south have two. Except where the land is watered by the farmer as well as by rain, only one crop can be grown in a year in the north. In the south-west two crops can be grown because of the two rainy seasons.

Exercises

1. Prepare a chart to show how farmers in your school area use their time in the 12 months of the year. Is there any relationship between the chart and the climate of the area?
2. Prepare a graph using the rainfall figures given below. Follow the example of the graphs above.

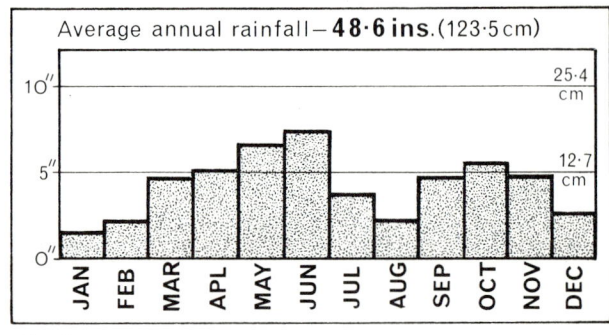

Aburi

Rainfall figures in inches (multiply these figures by 2.5 for approximate equivalent in centimetres)

Towns	Jan	Feb	Mar	Apr	May	June	July	Aug	Sept	Oct	Nov	Dec	Total
Bolgatanga	0·1	0·2	0·7	1·9	4·2	5·7	6·9	9·7	8·6	2·6	0·5	0·1	41·2
Wenchi	0·3	1·8	3·4	5·7	7·0	8·3	3·7	2·6	7·9	9·0	3·2	0·7	53·6
Axim	2·1	2·4	5·1	5·6	16·5	21·1	6·2	2·1	3·4	8·1	7·6	3·8	84·0
Mampong (Ashanti)	0·3	2·8	5·7	6·2	8·2	7·1	5·4	2·1	5·3	8·5	4·3	0·4	56·3

6. Rivers and Lakes

The river at Dwinasi

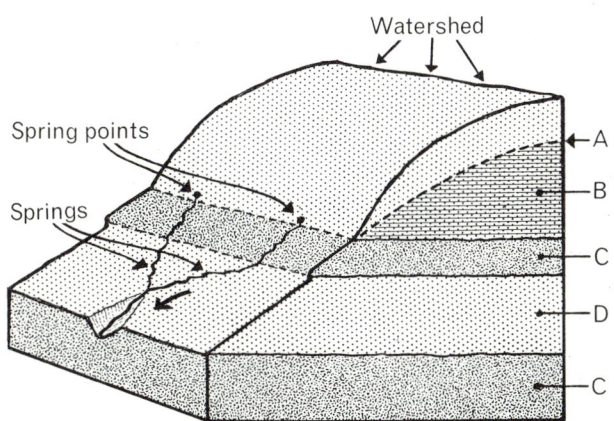

A. Water table (it falls in the dry season and rises in the wet season)
B. Porous rock containing rainwater
C. Impervious rock
D. Porous rock

Cross-section of a watershed

Rivers and lakes are very important to man. In Ghana rivers and streams are the main sources of water. Some people depend on rivers and lakes for a living; they catch fish which they sell. They also travel on rivers and lakes from one part of the country to another. In the past some Ghanaians obtained gold from the stream-beds. This was very important because it was gold which brought some of the early Europeans to our country to trade. (Even today the Bremang Gold Dredging Company obtains some gold from the bed of the river Ofin.)

Electricity is produced from swift-flowing rivers by using the power of the water. Where a river does not flow fast enough a *dam*, or wall, can be built to help. Water collects behind the dam and then falls suddenly to a lower level. It provides the power which is needed to turn the heavy machines and produce *hydro-electricity* ('hydro' means water). This is what has been done to the Volta at Akosombo.

Rivers and streams come from rain. When it rains some of the water sinks into the ground if the rocks of the area are *porous* and have very small holes in them which let the water through. Below the porous rocks may be other hard rocks which slope and are not porous. (See the diagram opposite.) Underground water flows on the hard rocks until it appears at the surface somewhere as a spring. This may be joined by other springs to form a river. The lands from which streams and rivers flow are usually high and are known as *watersheds* or *water partings*.

The principal watersheds of Ghana are the Gambaga scarp and the Koforidua-Wenchi scarp (part of which is known as the Kwahu scarp). The main watershed of the Volta river is outside Ghana in Upper Volta. It is from this that the Black Volta flows. Underground water upon which the flow of rivers depends can be lost through *evaporation*. This is when the water dries and turns back to vapour (see page 11). To reduce this and allow rivers to flow without ceasing, some forest reserves have been created. Other reasons for reserving forest in Ghana will be mentioned later.

The important rivers in Ghana are the Volta, the Pra, the Ankobra and the Tano. (Look back

Two vehicles of transport on Lake Volta: a car ferry and a local canoe

to the map on page 5.) The Volta is the longest, and stretches for over 1,000 miles (1,600 km) from its source to its mouth. You can see from the map that it starts as the Black Volta and flows north-eastwards until it comes to the north-west corner of Ghana. It turns southwards, then eastwards and southwards again until it enters the sea at Ada.

The Volta has three main *tributaries*, or smaller rivers which flow into it. These are the Afram, the Oti and the Red Volta. In most places, the Volta is shallow with very gentle banks. The result of this is that the river usually overflows its banks in the rainy season and destroys property, especially farms and houses.

In spite of this, the Volta is a very useful river. It is used for *transport* and fishing. Its greatest benefit is the electricity which it provides. There are plans to use it for watering part of the Accra Plains, by digging small channels across the land for the river to flow into. This is called *irrigation*.

West of the Volta is the river Pra, which also has three main tributaries. They are the Ofin, the Anum and the Birim. The beds of the Pra and its tributaries have some gold *deposits*. Many people living in these areas used to dig for gold. We can still find many gold-mining pits in parts drained by the rivers. The Ofin river was also used for floating logs to Dunkwa, a railway station. From there they were taken by train to the coast for export abroad.

The Ankobra, whose main tributaries are the Mansi and the Bonsa, is a much shorter river. In its upper parts the current of the river flows very swiftly, creating *rapids*. In the past its lower section was used to carry mining machinery from the coast to some of the nearby mining areas. The Tano, the last of the important rivers, was used by small launches to travel from the coast to Tanoso.

Ghana now has two main lakes: Lake Bosumtwi, a natural lake, and Lake Volta, an artificial one. We shall talk about the artificial lake later. Lake Bosumtwi, with an area of about $18\frac{1}{2}$ square miles

Irrigation channels carry water from the rivers to the rice fields

(46 sq. km), is in Ashanti, to the south-south-east of Kumasi. The lake occupies a big hole made by a volcano, which caused a violent explosion, shooting out pieces of rock from the earth's crust and leaving a hollow called a *crater*. The lake is surrounded by about 24 villages and is important for fishing. The people of the villages send their catch of fish to Kumasi, Betwai and Kokofu for sale.

The lake also attracts some visitors. But, because of poor transport and the steep footpath from the top of the lake, not many tourists are able to reach the lake shore.

Exercises
1. Name four important rivers in Africa. Use an atlas.
2. In each case mention the river's main uses.
3. Explain why many small rivers in Ghana stop flowing in the dry season.

Logs are floated downriver to Takoradi

7. Vegetation

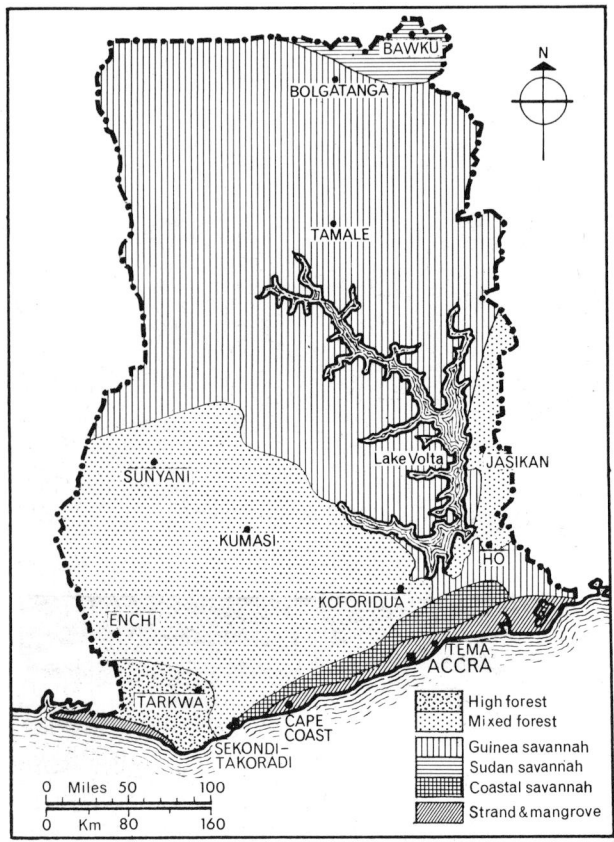

The vegetation of Ghana

Outside our towns, villages and farms, and on roads and paths, we often do not see the bare earth. It is mostly covered by vegetation. *Vegetation* means plants which grow on their own (without anybody helping them). Such plants are different from crops, for example, rice, millet and cocoa, which are grown by man for food or to be sold for money to buy other things.

There are two main types of vegetation in Ghana. (See the map opposite.) These are *forest* and *savannah*. There is also a small area of *strand* and *mangrove*. The forests are mainly in the south-west part of the country where the rainfall is heavy and there is a short dry season. The savannah is mainly in the north, where the rains are less heavy and the dry season is long. Areas with savannah vegetation suffer from great *evaporation*, when much surface and underground water is lost to the atmosphere.

Climate is one important factor which affects vegetation. Another factor which can make vegetation grow well or prevent it from doing so is soil. For example, in some coastal areas the narrow strip of land bordering the sea does not have tall trees. There is sufficient water but the soil contains salt from the sea. The vegetation here is strand and mangrove, which is

Map legend:
- High forest
- Mixed forest
- Guinea savannah
- Sudan savannah
- Coastal savannah
- Strand & mangrove

Mixed forest at Dwinasi

Young trees for the forest reserves are grown in special nurseries

a mixture of creeping plants and grass. This type of vegetation can grow in soils which contain salt.

We now know of two factors which affect vegetation. These are climate and soil. There is a third factor: animals and man. Animals and man can destroy the vegetation of a place and so prevent it from developing properly. Burning and cutting timber are some of the ways in which man destroys vegetation.

Now let us look at the two main types of vegetation more closely.

Forests

The forest vegetation may be divided into two kinds. These are *high forest* and *mixed forest*. The high forest is in the south-west of the country where the rainfall is heavy, about 70 inches (178 cm) or more. The forest is dense with tall trees, which generally keep their leaves all through the year. They are called *evergreen*. In some areas

the land is flat and there is a lot of water which is not able to drain away. Raphia palms and bamboos grow on this wet land. Mixed forest covers a wider area than high forest. The trees in mixed forest are also tall but most of them are not evergreen. At different times of year they *shed* (drop) their leaves. Both here and in the rain forest area the branches and leaves of the trees are in layers (or *canopies*). They look like umbrellas arranged one on top of the other.

Forests are very useful to Ghanaians. They provide timber which is used for building houses and making furniture. Some of it is sent abroad. Canoes, carvings such as *oware*, and stools are made from some forest trees. Some forests are now *reserves*, so that the country may always have products from her forests, especially timber. The trees in the reserves are not to be cut for making farms and permission is needed to enter the reserves.

Taking measurements of ground levels in the savannah area

In the forests other plants are grown for their products. Cocoa is cultivated, and another important tree is the oil palm.

Savannah

This type of vegetation covers a very large area of Ghana indeed. It consists of grass mixed with trees. There are more trees in the south than in the north.

There are three main types of savannah. They are *Guinea savannah*, *Sudan savannah* and *coastal savannah*.

1. *Guinea savannah.* This is the largest of the three areas and contains a number of trees. It is believed that many years ago there were more trees. They are now few and look poorer because the grass is often burnt down.

2. *Sudan savannah.* This type is found in the north-east where trees are fewer and smaller. One of the common plants is *acacia*.

3. *Coastal savannah.* This lies between the mixed forest and the strand and mangrove along the coast. The area widens eastwards from Takoradi. The rainfall is low, about 30 inches (76 cm) a year

in the Accra area. The vegetation is mainly grass with shrubs and groups of bushes.

The savannah areas are of great value to Ghana. Cows and sheep are kept here and provide some of the country's beef and mutton. Such cereals as guinea corn, millet and upland rice are grown in the savannahs in the north. Shea butter, used for food and as pomade (a dressing for the skin and hair), also comes from the north. In the coastal savannahs, vegetables, for example tomatoes, onions, garden eggs and pepper, are cultivated.

Exercises

1. Draw a tree with three canopies. The photograph on page 16 will help you.
2. Give two reasons why there are forest reserves in Ghana.
3. How can animals affect or change the vegetation of an area?

8. Cocoa

Most Ghanaians are farmers and they grow many crops. One of the most important crops is *cocoa*. This crop yields beans which are sent abroad to be sold to other countries. This is known as *exporting*. With the money paid by countries which buy (*import*) the beans, Ghanaians are able to purchase some of the things they do not produce themselves. When the price of cocoa is high Ghana gets a great deal of money. Cocoa is grown to be sold for money and not to be eaten by the farmers and their families, so it is what is called a *cash crop*. Ghana's cocoa is bought by Great Britain, the United States of America, West Germany, Japan, the Netherlands and Russia.

Cocoa was introduced to Ghana by a Ghanaian called Tetteh Quashie in 1879. Quashie went to the island of Fernando Po in 1870 and brought some cocoa beans back with him when he returned to Ghana. He first grew cocoa at Mampong on the Akwapim Ridge. Before Tetteh Quashie other people had tried to bring the crop into the country. Some of them were the Basel missionaries in 1857 and 1861, but unfortunately they did not succeed.

From the Akwapim area the crop quickly spread to the Densu and Birim basins. It later reached Ashanti, Brong Ahafo and other parts of the forest areas of Ghana.

Cocoa grows very well in certain conditions. The rainfall should be between 45 and 75 inches (115–190 cm) a year, and it should fall throughout the whole year. The crop will not grow and give good yields if all the rain falls in four to five months, leaving the rest of the year dry. There must also be moisture in the air (the humidity must be high). Cocoa does not like harmattan winds, which are dry. To prevent these winds from harming the cocoa crop, forest reserves are built in their path as a barrier. These reserves are along the northern boundary of the forest zone.

Each cocoa tree has about 20 pods

Women collecting the ripe cocoa pods. The crop is harvested in November

Cocoa likes shade, especially the young trees. Farmers therefore leave some of the forest trees when they are clearing the ground for their cocoa farms. Where there are not many trees, farmers may plant more. Some food crops grown with cocoa provide a shade, but this is only for a short period.

Cocoa also likes well-drained rich soils, with plenty of *humus* which is made by dead leaves. Many farmers have a way of knowing whether the soil of a place is good for cocoa. They can tell from the colour of the soil or the presence of some plants. But the best way to know whether the soil of a place is good for cocoa is to ask the Ministry of Agriculture, which offers free advice to farmers about soils and other matters.

There are two main types of cocoa grown in Ghana. They are the Amelonado and the Amazonia. Amelonado has small pods with many beans, and takes five to seven years before it starts to yield. Amazonia begins to produce pods much earlier, after about three years. The pods are large but contain fewer beans.

Cocoa is very important to the Ghanaians. It gives many farmers their *income* (the money they obtain from their work) for the year. With the money received they are able to pay the school fees of their children, buy clothes to wear, and look after their families.

Since 1950 the Ghana Cocoa Marketing Board has been buying and selling Ghanaian cocoa. It has been able to make money, some of which has been used to build schools, roads and clinics. The C.M.B. also offers scholarships. The Government receives part of the money cocoa brings. It does so through the taxes the farmers pay. The money the Government receives is used to provide services (schools, hospitals, roads, etc.) throughout the whole country.

The diagram on page 21 shows you the importance of cocoa in the country's exports, and the quantity of cocoa that is produced.

The cultivation of cocoa is responsible for much *migration* in Ghana. Many people have left their home towns and have gone to live in the cocoa areas as farmers. There are many new villages in the cocoa areas. Some have grown to become towns with large populations.

Splitting open the cocoa pods to remove the beans

Drying the beans in the sun

The dry beans are poured into sacks for easy transport

Weighing the beans at a buying station

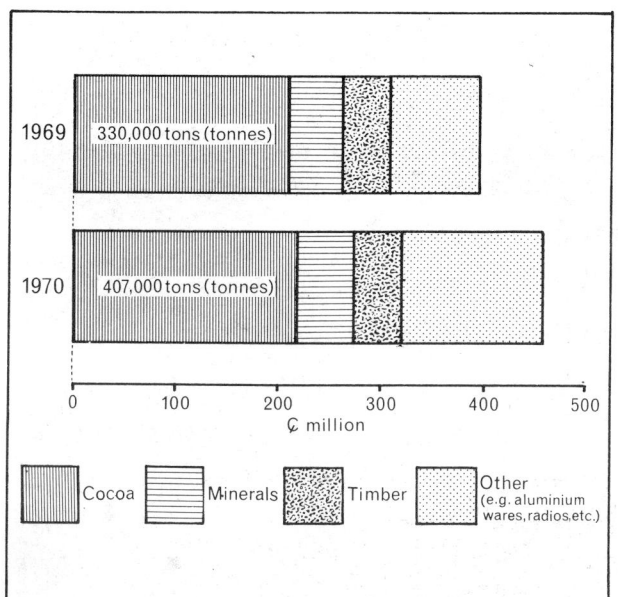

The main exports of Ghana

Close-up of a cocoa pod

Cocoa, like human beings, suffers from old age and disease. Because of this, some cocoa-growing areas, especially in the Eastern Region, are now almost without any cocoa trees. The most deadly disease is '*swollen shoot*', which is passed from tree to tree by an insect. The Government has been trying to control the disease, by destroying the trees that are diseased and asking farmers to spray their trees with special powder or liquid which will kill the insects.

Exercises

1. Draw a map of Ghana to show the main areas where cocoa is grown.
2. On your map show ten main towns which are cocoa markets.
3. What are the uses of cocoa?

A special funnel is inserted into the sack to sample the cocoa beans before marketing

Yaw Sabeng holding some swollen shoots. He was the first man to discover the disease

Government officials demonstrating sprays for controlling the insects that attack cocoa plants

9.   Producing for Local Factories

Cocoa is important. But it is not the only crop grown by Ghanaian farmers to earn a living. There are other crops produced for export, for example coffee. Some crops are grown for use in local factories. The most important of these are oil palm, limes, sugar cane and tobacco. Some of these crops have been grown for many years, but only to feed the farmers' families. Recently they have become important *raw materials* for local factories, which turn the crops into other products.

Oil palm
This plant gives palm nuts. Palm-oil comes from the soft outer part (the *pericarp*) of the palm nut. From the *kernel* of the palm nut, palm-kernel-oil comes. You can eat the oils from palm nuts, and the pericarp is used locally to make palm soup.

In some countries, palm-oil is used to make soap. The United Kingdom is one of these countries. Because she cannot grow her own palm trees she imports palm-oil from Nigeria and Malaya. Before cocoa became the main export crop, Ghana prepared and sold palm-oil to the United Kingdom. The industry is important in the southern part of the forest zone where the oil palm tree grows.

The oil palm is now grown to give large quantities of nuts for palm-oil factories. One of these factories is at Sese in the Western Region. There are other places in the forest area where new farms have been made to produce palm nuts for palm-oil factories. The Government has helped by bringing good nuts with a thick pericarp from southern Nigeria, to be grown in other areas.

Young oil-palm plants

Harvesting the palm nuts

Limes

Limes are grown in the Asebu-Asuansi area. An important town in the lime-growing area is Abakrampa. Like cocoa, limes were brought into Ghana from another country. They came from the West Indies in 1913 and were planted at the Asuansi Agricultural Station. In 1928 Rose Limited, a lime juice company, built a factory and made large lime plantations. The company obtains many of the limes it uses from its plantations. Asebu farmers also grow limes and sell them to the Rose company to make lime juice. The lime juice is then exported and sold to many foreign countries.

Sugar cane

Not many years ago this crop was grown for chewing only. Children love it because of its sugary juice. Now it is cultivated in some parts of Ghana as a raw material for sugar factories. The sugar factories are at Komenda and Asutsuare, where there are large sugar cane plantations. Some of the canes are bought from private farmers. Sugar cane is a tropical crop and likes a lot of rain.

Tobacco

This is another crop which has been grown in Ghana for some years. Its leaves are used to make cigarettes, cigars and smoker's tobacco. Tobacco used to be exported. Great improvements began in 1952 when the Pioneer Tobacco Company was formed. The company supplied seedlings from its own nurseries to help the farmers to produce healthy tobacco. Farmers now grow their own seedlings. The seeds are sown in raised beds to protect them from heavy rainfall and to allow the farmer to walk between the rows. Later the seedlings are transplanted, or moved, and again grown on ridges, as the tobacco plant is very delicate and needs to be protected.

The main areas where tobacco is grown are Northern Ashanti, Brong Ahafo, Northern Ghana and the Volta Region.

Exercises

1. Name three products that are made from oil palm nuts.
2. What are the conditions suitable for the cultivation of sugar cane?

A sugar cane plantation

A tobacco plantation. Notice the raised beds

24

10. Commercial Food Farming

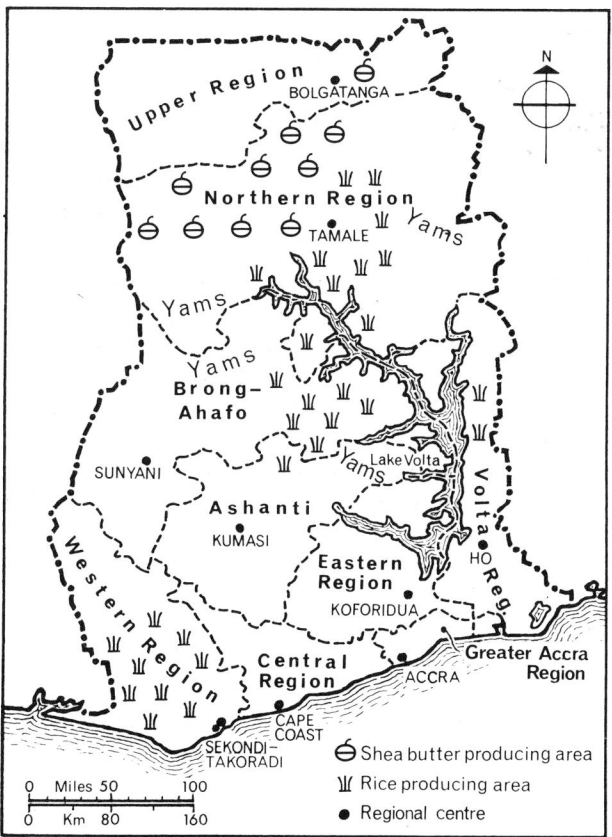

The agricultural products of Ghana

There are two kinds of food production in Ghana. Some people produce food to feed themselves. These are *subsistence farmers*. They sell what they are unable to use. Other people have large farms and grow food crops mainly to sell. They use only a small part of the crop to feed themselves and their family and sell the rest. These are *commercial farmers*.

More people are now beginning to grow food for sale because the number of people in Ghana (the population) is increasing. Also the number of people living in large towns and doing non-farming work is rising. Even in the small towns not many people grow their own food.

Almost all the food crops in Ghana can be grown in large quantities to be sold commercially. Around many of the large towns there are villages, and some of the villagers produce foodstuffs to sell to the people in the towns. In some of the villages around Kumasi there are farmers who grow cassava, maize and cocoyams for sale in Kumasi. On the Accra Plains the important crops are maize and vegetables, such as peppers, garden eggs, okro etc.

Two main crops which are often grown in large quantities are *white yams* and *rice*. White yams are grown in Northern Ashanti, Brong Ahafo, Krachi, Wa and Gonja. The soil in these

Weeding rows of cassava

The ripe maize crop

places is light and sandy. It is easy to make mounds in which the *tubers*, or yam plants, can grow. Yams may be grown with millet, guinea corn and groundnuts. Some yam farmers are able to grow thousands of yams. They sell them to *food contractors*. Food contractors buy crops from the farmers and sell them to the shops and markets, so that the farmer does not himself go to market.

Most Ghanaians like yams and eat a lot of them. But the growing of yams has become more profitable because some are now exported to the United Kingdom where there are many Africans studying or working.

The important rice-growing areas are Ahanta Nzima, Buem and parts of north Ghana. There are two types of rice. *Upland rice* is grown on the slopes of hills and does not need much water. *Paddy rice* needs a lot of water, and it is grown in valley bottoms where the water collects. The principal area for paddy rice is Ahanta Nzima in the south-west, and it is also grown in parts of the north.

Rice-growing in north Ghana has increased in recent years. Farmers are able to make large farms. They do so by using ploughs drawn by oxen. The way of removing the husks, or skin, from the rice must be improved so that more Ghanaians can buy it. If this happens, less rice will need to be imported from other countries.

Tending the young rice plants

Ploughing the rice fields

Yam tubers are planted inside these mounds

Exercises
1. Draw a map of Ghana. Find on it your local council centre. Find the places from which this centre gets its foodstuffs. Mark the places on the map. Join them to the local council centre by lines.
2. Why are there more commercial farmers now than in the past?

11. Improving Agriculture

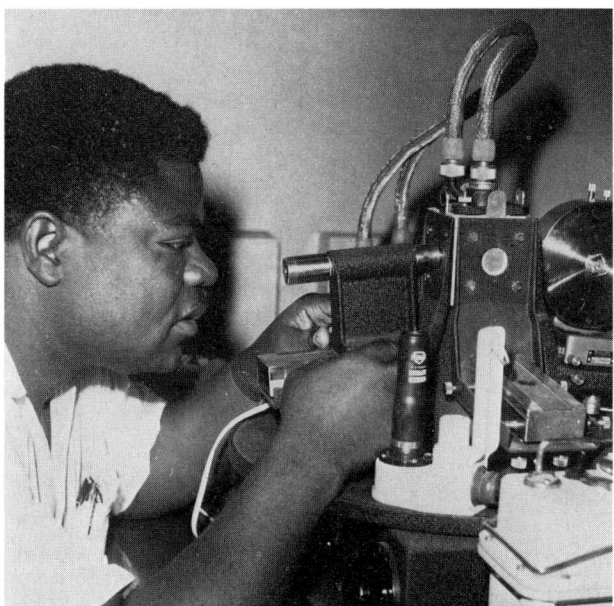

A research scientist studying soil samples

A student at a government agricultural school tending a cocoa plant seedling

Ghana is an *agricultural* country which means that most Ghanaians earn their living by farming. About 70 per cent (70 out of every 100) of the people work in agriculture. Some people now work in factories, but for some time to come most workers will be employed on the farms.

Two important natural factors needed for successful agriculture are good soil and plenty of water. Ghana has rich soil in some places; in other areas the soil is not so rich, or *fertile*. All kinds of soil are being studied in order to know what to grow on them, and how to treat them so that they may produce more crops than at present. Soils begin to lose their richness if they are used for too long. Manure and *artificial fertilizers* are used to put back some of the goodness into the soil. Suitable manures and fertilizers are continually being studied.

The rainfall of Ghana is different from place to place (see Chapter 5). More rain falls in the south-west and centre of the country, but not so much in the south-east and north. The difference is seen in the crops grown. Studies are being made of the rainfall to develop more suitable types of crops, which will grow better in the various kinds of climate and give greater yields.

It is necessary to improve the country's agriculture for four main reasons. First, Ghana will have more to sell to other people if she produces more. Second, the population of Ghana is increasing; Ghana must produce more to feed the increasing number of its citizens. Third, the *bush fallow system* is becoming out of date. This is a system of clearing an area, working on it for two or three years and then leaving it to go back to bush and moving to a fresh piece of land. Under this system the land that has been farmed is able to regain its fertility only if left undisturbed for a long time—about ten years. Because of the increase in population, more land is needed and the bush fallow system is not possible in many places. Instead, fertilizers and manure are used on the soil and the crops are rotated. *Crop rotation* means growing a different crop each year so that the soil is not always used in the same way. The soil stays fertile, and there is no need to leave the land fallow to regain its fertility. Finally, our method of farming has to

Young farmers at the Wenchi Farm Institute learning how to drive a tractor

change so that less work is needed to grow crops in a small area. The farmer can then work a larger area and produce more crops. Tractors and other machines help the farmer to work faster and more easily.

Some modernization of Ghana's agriculture has already started. In the Northern and Upper Regions, farmers use animals to plough the land. The State Farms Corporation has tractors which it uses to plough its farms before cultivation.

Two institutions which have been helping to modernize Ghanaian agriculture are the Agriculture Department and the Agricultural Research Institute at Kwadaso. The Institute has stations at Manya in the Upper Region, Nyankpala in the Northern Region, and Aiyiasi and Princes Town in the Western Region. Other stations are at Ejura in Ashanti, and Pokoase and Tafo in the Eastern Region.

Exercises

1. How do farmers make their soil fertile in your village?
2. What method is used to help keep the soil of your school garden fertile?
3. What is the bush fallow system? What are its advantages and disadvantages?

Agricultural shows exhibit new equipment and methods. They are held regularly in the Volta Region

12. Products of the North

Millet plants

Sheep arriving at the market

The exports of Ghana come mainly from the southern part of the country. But north Ghana also plays an important part. Ghanaians from the north help to produce cocoa, the chief export crop.

Some products from the north have already been mentioned. They are rice, tobacco and yams. Other products which are important in the north are millet, guinea corn, groundnuts, shea butter and cattle. These are some of the main items of *internal trade*. They are produced in the north and sent to other parts of the country for sale.

Millet and guinea corn are grown in gardens around compounds and on farms in the bush. Like cow peas, hibiscus, soup plants and many other vegetables, they are grown mainly for home use. But some farmers produce more than they need, and the surplus is offered for sale in the north and in towns in the southern part of the country.

Millet and guinea corn are grown on narrow ridges about six inches (15 cm) high with channels between the ridges to take away rainwater. The seeds are planted in March. Millet is harvested in July and early August and guinea corn is harvested in October or early November.

Shea butter is another product from the north. It is prepared from the fruit of the shea butter tree, which is a *natural resource* because it grows by itself. It usually grows to a height of between 10 and 20 feet (3–6 metres), but some can reach 50 feet (15 metres). The fruits fall from the tree and are collected by women and children. The 'butter' is made from the fruit. Shea butter is used as pomade, fuel and for cooking.

Ghana has a number of different kinds of livestock. They are cattle, sheep, goats, pigs, donkeys, horses and poultry. Most of these provide food which gives us *protein*. Protein builds our bodies and helps to repair damaged skin or broken bones. The most important of these animals as food are cattle, sheep and goats, about three-quarters of which come from north Ghana. The remaining quarter come from the Accra Plains, the Volta Region and around Cape Coast.

Many cattle, sheep and goats are reared in the north because there is grass there, and there are not many tsetse flies. Many chiefs have large herds of cattle, sometimes about 400 animals, and herdsmen take these animals to the fields for grazing. Most people have quite small numbers of cattle—between two and ten animals. Children often take the cattle to the fields to feed.

The map opposite shows you the parts of the north where there are many animals, and the *cattle routes* of Ghana. These are paths along which the cattle are taken from the north to other parts of the country. The cattle in the picture below will travel about 400 miles (640 km) to reach Accra. On the map you can also see Bolgatanga which has a meat factory where corned beef is made.

The cattle in Ghana cannot provide all the beef which Ghanaians need. Ghana, therefore, imports cattle from other West African countries.

Exercises

1. Draw a sketch map of West Africa, and show on it the countries from which Ghana gets part of its meat supply.
2. Why are cattle generally scarce in the forest areas of Ghana?

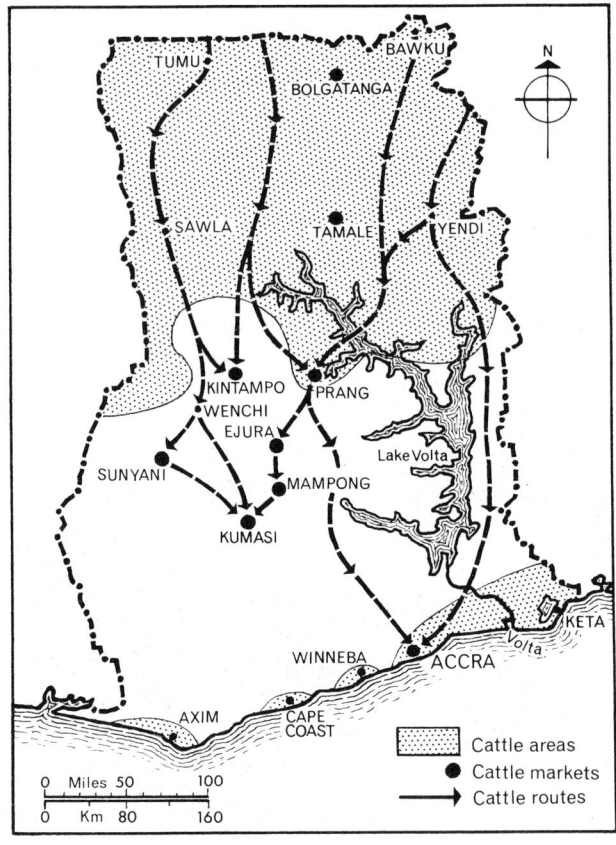

The cattle routes of Ghana

Cattle grazing in the northern savannah

30

The cattle route from the north to Accra

13. Fishing

A deep-sea fishing boat returning to port. Notice the large sail

Fishing is one of the chief occupations of the people living along the coast. They catch fish in the sea and lagoons. Some people also fish in rivers and lakes. River fishing is done in the Volta and some of the other main rivers, and in Lake Bosumtwi in Ashanti.

Sea fishing is done with two special kinds of net. A *seine net* is long. One end of it is held by a rope on the shore. Fishermen in a boat take the net, cast it in a semi-circle and bring the other end to another part of the shore. The men then drag in the net to catch the fish that are trapped in the semi-circle.

Drift nets are taken out to sea, some miles away from the shore. They are cast from canoes, which generally have sails and move with the aid of the wind.

In shallow water, for example in lagoons, *cast nets* are used. These are round and have weights around the edge. They also have strings in the middle. The fisherman holds the strings to cast the net. There are also other ways to catch fish, crabs, lobsters, etc. in small quantities from rivers and lagoons. Some are caught in small baskets which are hung in the water.

Sea fishing is *seasonal*. It is only done at certain times of year when the fish are fully grown and ready to eat. It starts in March or April and ends in September or October. During the fishing season some fishermen may travel to other places. Some Ghanaian fishermen are now living in other parts of West Africa, for example the Ivory Coast.

Many Ghanaian shores are busy during the fishing season. Women go to buy fish which they sell in the markets. Often Ghanaian children go to help so that they may be given fish to take home.

Drawing in the large seine net at Cape Coast

Some of the fish are sold fresh. But large quantities are *cured* before being sold. Some of the methods of curing fish are smoking, salting and drying. Cured fish keep longer.

The Ghanaian Government has been trying to improve upon the methods of fishing and selling fish. Fishing boats are now built at Sekondi. The new boats are bigger and are driven by *diesel* (oil) or petrol engines. They are suitable for *deep-sea fishing* which is how herrings are caught.

Some of the ports used by modern fishing vessels are Tema, Takoradi and Elmina.

The Ghana Fishing Corporation buys fish in large quantities from local and foreign fishing companies and sells it fresh throughout the country.

Exercises

1. How are fish cured in Ghana? Give details of the different methods.
2. What are the main activities in a fishing village?
3. Find out as much as you can about methods of fishing in other countries. Write a short description of each method.

Throwing a cast net needs careful balance

14. Mining

Boring for gold

Mining first attracted Europeans to the coast of Ghana in the fifteenth century. Even before this date some traders from the Mediterranean coast came to Ghana and other parts of West Africa to find gold.

Ghanaians mined the gold and sold it to the Europeans and other traders. European miners took even more interest in gold mining in the nineteenth century. They bought land and obtained permission to look for gold in the Tarkwa-Prestea-Aboso area. Later, gold was also mined at Obuasi, Bibiani and Konongo. Gold mining still takes place at Tarkwa, Prestea and Obuasi. (See the map opposite.)

Other minerals which are mined in Ghana are diamonds, manganese and bauxite. Diamonds are mined in the Akwatia-Oda area. The mining is done by the Consolidated African Selections Trust Limited, which is a private company, and the Ghana States Mining Corporation, which belongs to the Government. Many Africans have also been permitted by the Government to look for diamonds. Ghana diamonds are used mainly for *industrial* purposes. They are very hard and are used to cut materials such as glass.

The mineral deposits of Ghana

Legend:
- ⊙ Gold
- ◇ Diamond
- ▲ Bauxite
- Ⅰ Iron ore
- ▣ Manganese
- ⏚ Oil (prospecting)
- + Production in progress

Locations: SHIENI, Lake Volta, NYINAHIN, KONONGO, OBUASI, NKAWKAW, KIBI, BIBIANI, AWASO, AKWATIA, PRESTEA, DUNKWA, ODA, BONSASO, TARKWA, NSUTA

Scale: 0 Miles 50 100 / 0 Km 80 160

Washing diamond-bearing gravel

Separating diamonds from sand by hand

Bauxite at Takoradi harbour before export

Manganese is mined at Nsuta, near Tarkwa. It is exported and used to make hard steel and batteries. Bauxite mining began in the Second World War (1939–45) at Awaso. Aluminium comes from bauxite. It is used to make a number of very important things, such as ships, aeroplanes, pans, roofing sheets and window frames. Aluminium is particularly useful in the tropics because it does not rust. Ghana has great deposits of bauxite near Nyinahin, 40 miles (64 km) west of Kumasi, at Awaso, Mount Ejuanema, two miles (3 km) from Nkawkaw, near the River Bia, 40 miles (64 km) north-west of Wiawso, and near Kibi, 55 miles (88 km) north-west of Accra. At present, the main source is Awaso.

VALCO (the Volta Aluminium Company) manufactures aluminium from imported bauxite, using hydro-electric power from the Volta. One day aluminium will be obtained from locally-mined bauxite and will no longer need to be imported.

Another mineral is salt, which is an important item of food. Most of the salt comes from salt-water lagoons. The water evaporates, or dries up, leaving the salt as a thin film on the sides of the lagoon. In a good year, that is when the rains are not heavy and the lakes dry up, about 5,000 to 6,000 tons (tonnes) of salt may be collected. Near

Weija, Accra, the Panbros Company manufactures salt by trapping seawater in shallow tanks and evaporating it. It is estimated that Ghana can produce about 125,000 tons (tonnes) of sea salt annually by using more suitable methods. A little salt is also obtained from sandy soil at Daboya, about 20 miles (32 km) west of Tamale.

There is some petroleum in Ghana. It is found off-shore at Saltpond. Prospectors are attempting to discover if the mineral is present in large quantities.

With the exception of salt, almost all the minerals produced in Ghana are exported for *foreign exchange* (money from other countries). Ghana greatly needs money from abroad to be able to buy some of the things Ghanaians need and cannot produce locally. Mining also provides jobs for people. For these two reasons the Government is greatly worried when mineral output falls.

Exercises
1. What are the uses of gold and diamonds?
2. Name three towns which are no longer important for gold mining.
3. Name an important mining town and describe how mining has affected the life of the people who live there.

34

15. Power

Power is the energy which lights many homes, drives machines in factories, and in some countries moves trains, ships, lorries and cars. In Ghana it is mainly the large towns and mining areas which have power.

Until very recently, most of the large towns got their power from oil, which helped to turn machines to *generate*, or produce, the power. This method is still in use in some places. In small villages some people have their own *generators* which look like small machines. Some mining companies, before using oil, used firewood to obtain power. Fires provided steam which turned machines and generated power.

Now the Volta is the main source of power in Ghana. It provides hydro-electricity, which we have described earlier in Chapter 6. The amount of power which the Volta produces is very great. The pictures will help you understand how the dam operates.

A large part of it is bought and used by the Volta Aluminium Company (VALCO) in its factory at Tema. Some of the rest is used in other factories, especially in the large towns—Accra, Tema, Kumasi and Takoradi—and also in homes. Ghana can produce more electricity at Akosombo, and has agreed to sell power to Togo and Dahomey.

The hydro-electric power produced at Akosombo is very important for the economic development of the country. Ghana needs industries, for which cheap power is essential.

To produce hydro-electricity at Akosombo, the Volta Lake was artificially created. It covers an area of over 3,000 square miles (7,500 sq. km), and there is enough water to supply much of Ghana with power. The lake now has two principal uses, as well as providing a regular supply of power. It is used for fishing and transport. It may later help the cultivation of rice, improve the water supply,

The force of the water overflowing to a lower level generates hydro-electricity

and even affect the climate by making the rainfall in certain parts of the land around it more reliable. This is because winds blow the water off the lake, as they do off the sea, and carry it over the land.

The Volta Lake has affected many villages which were once close to the river Volta. About 58 villages and the farms around them have been covered by the lake. The people in the villages affected have been moved to new villages in different parts of the country.

Water flows through these narrow channels to the lower part of the lake

Exercises

1. Find on the map six new villages built for some of the people affected by the Volta Lake.
2. Find two ports on the Volta Lake.
3. Draw a sketch map of Africa and show on it six important rivers which provide hydro-electricity. Mark the places on the rivers where the power is generated.

This picture shows the turbines being put into position when the dam was built. You can see the blades which are turned by the force of the water to drive the generators

16. Craft Industries

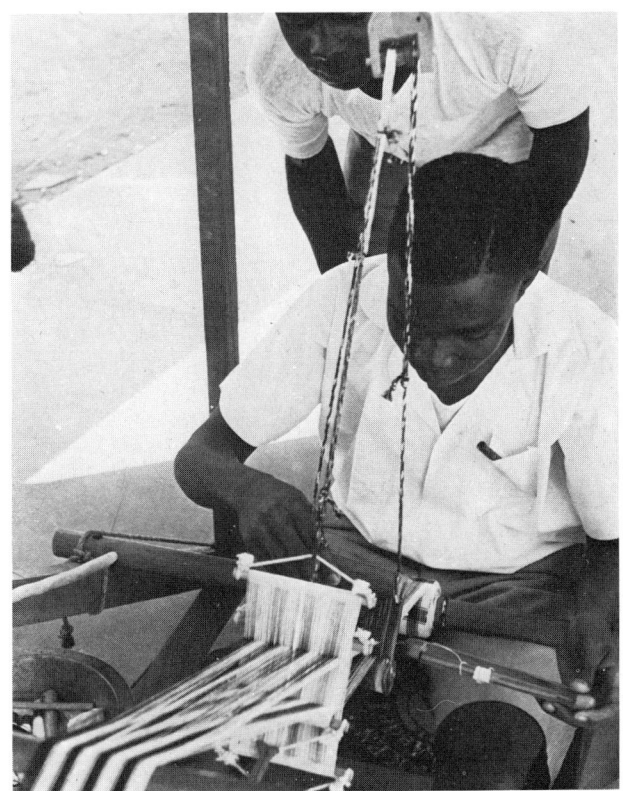

Weaving kente cloth on a small handloom

You have all seen kente, fugu (smocks), stools, baskets, pots, mats, saddles, slippers and cushions. These are some of the products of the craft industries of Ghana. Simple hand tools were used to make them in the past. Today machines and other tools are also used to help produce articles more cheaply and easily.

Craft industries can be organized by single individuals or by groups of people. For some crafts the materials are cheap but for others, such as goldsmithery, kente-weaving, boat and canoe-making, a great deal more money is required. The money is needed to buy modern machinery and raw materials.

Some industries belong to certain areas. For example, weaving is done in Bonwire. Some industries are placed in areas where raw materials can be obtained quickly. For example, canoe-making is carried on near forests, where wood can easily be obtained. Others, such as carving in Kumasi, are in places where there are many people who will buy the products.

Kente

Long ago most of the cloths worn by Ghanaians were produced locally on handlooms. Now Ghanaians wear machine-woven cloths (*textiles*) which are either imported or come from the textile factories at Tema and Akosombo.

But many people still want kente cloth to wear on social occasions. There are two main areas where kente is woven in Ghana. These are the villages on the north of the Keta Lagoon and those to the east of Kumasi. Bonwire, Wono and Ampa are some of the villages near Kumasi. Weaving is done in the houses. The price of the cloth varies from ₵60 to ₵300. The cloth is expensive if the thread is of a very high quality and if the pattern is complicated.

Wood carving

One of the main products of wood carving are stools. Most chiefs in south Ghana, Ashanti and Brong Ahafo have stools. Not many ordinary stools are used in homes now. They are being replaced by chairs made by carpenters.

Some Ghanaians still carve. They produce small figures of animals and men, and other objects

Woodcarver at work on a stool

Making a simple basket

A finished basket

which are used to decorate rooms and are sold to tourists. There are some carvers in Kumasi and in Ahwia, a few miles away from Kumasi. The main raw materials are mahogany and other hard woods.

Basket and leather work

Baskets are among the common products made by schoolchildren in their craft lessons. They are made from palm branches, canes and grass. Baskets have many uses. They are used by cocoa farmers, maize, rice and millet growers, and by women for shopping.

Villages which specialize in the making of cane baskets are Asaman and Enyiresi on the Kumasi-Accra road. Another town noted for the production of cane baskets is Asamankese.

Grass baskets are made in the north, and many are brought to the south for sale.

Leather products are made in the north out of sheepskins and cow-hides. They include saddles, slippers, boots, cushions and seats.

Exercises

1. Draw a sketch map of Ghana and locate on it all the places mentioned in this chapter.
2. What are the craft industries of your area? How do the craftsmen work and what do they make?

Sandals, carvings and cloth on sale in the market

17. The Large Factories of Ghana

Not very long ago Ghanaians obtained almost all *manufactured goods* (goods produced in large factories) from outside, for example the United Kingdom, the United States of America and Japan. These goods included cloth for school uniforms, chalk, erasers, exercise books, cement, cars etc. The craft industries produced kente and a few other things needed in the home. Also from small workshops came clothes made by tailors and seamstresses, and furniture made by carpenters.

Now let us look at some of the reasons why Ghanaians were unable to produce goods in large factories: (1) Large factories need large sums of money. In the past there were not many wealthy Ghanaians with the courage to put their money into business. (2) Large factories often have complicated machinery which needs skill to handle and repair. Not many Ghanaians were skilled enough to do such work. (3) Ghana had not enough power to work the large machines in factories. (4) European manufacturers liked to produce goods in their own countries and send them abroad to sell.

Ghana now has a number of factories. (See the map below.) This is due to (1) Ghana's independence, (2) power from the Volta, (3) the encouragement given by the Government to people to open factories, and (4) the skill which Ghanaians are learning in the use of machinery. Also the Government itself builds new factories.

The three main areas with large factories in Ghana are Accra-Tema, Sekondi-Takoradi and Kumasi. These places have large populations, and can be reached quickly from most parts of the country. Tema and Takoradi are ports which import the raw materials needed in some of the factories in Ghana. From these places goods can be easily transported to local markets, and they can also be exported.

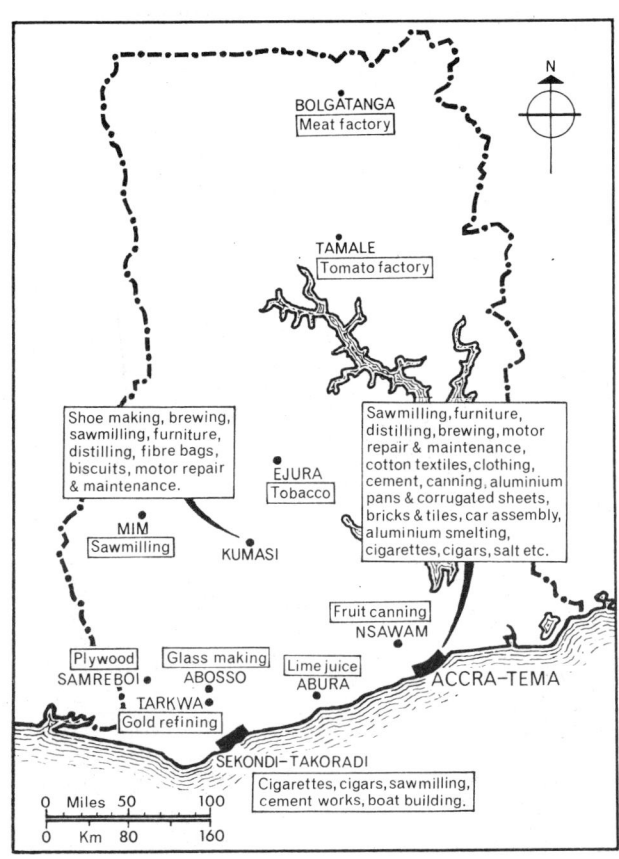

The main industries of Ghana

Volta Aluminium Company's new smelter at Tema

Molten aluminium which will later be cast into shape

Kumasi is near the centre of Ghana and in the densely populated part of Ashanti. It can be easily reached by road and railway, and its population makes it an important market.

There are many industries in Accra-Tema. They include furniture-making, brewing, textile manufacture, soap-making, chemical manufacture, boat-building, printing, flour-milling, aluminium-processing and the manufacture of aluminium articles. At Sekondi-Takoradi, cigarettes and cigars are made, and there are sawmills and boat-building yards; Kumasi has a brewery and sawmills, and its other industries include biscuit-making, and the manufacture of shoes and fibre bags. Some industries in other parts of Ghana are sugar-milling and refining at Komenda and Asutsuare, match-making at Kade, palm-oil manufacture at Sese, glass-making at Aboso, gold-refining at Tarkwa and meat-canning at Bolgatanga.

Weaving cloth from large spools of cotton. Compare this with the picture on page 37

Printing the finished cloth at the textile factory in Tema. The material passes under the inked rollers at the bottom

Welding in a shipyard

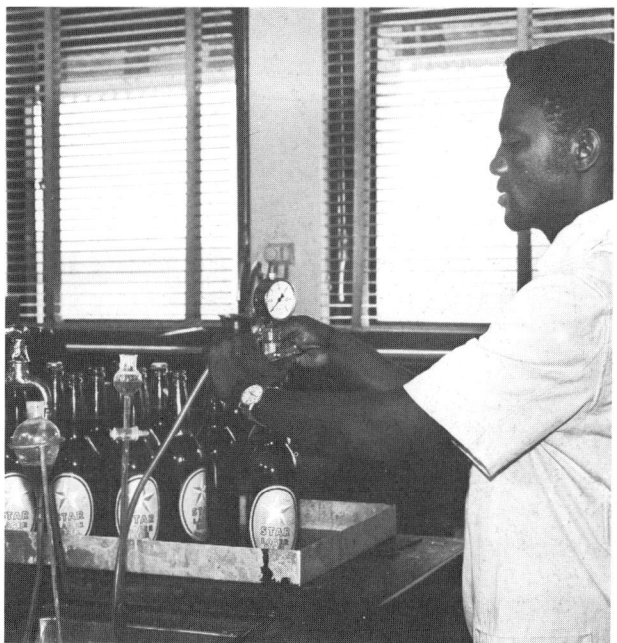

Checking beer at Kumasi Brewery

Sharpening the large saws at Dwinasi sawmill

Loading the sawn planks at Awaso

A sweet-making factory near Accra

Inspecting cosmetics at the factory in Jamestown

Finishing the stitching on mattresses at Tema

A modern control panel at Volta Aluminium Company

Many of the things produced are used in Ghana, but many of them are also exported. One of the ways of making goods which are manufactured in Ghana known throughout the world is through *trade fairs*. (See page 51.) The goods are also *advertised* in newspapers and on television.

More large factories are needed in Ghana. They will help to create jobs for young men and women who are leaving school. Modern industries need machines, but men are needed to service the machines, to organize the work and to advertise and sell the products.

Exercises

1. Take one industry of Ghana and write an essay about it. Some of the points you may consider are place, raw material, power, labour and how the products are sold.
2. What is your nearest local industry? Where do the raw materials come from and where is the finished product sold?

18.   How People Travel

It is very important today for businessmen to be able to send letters and telegrams quickly all over the world, and to be able to deliver goods quickly and easily. This is all part of what we call *communication*. People who govern the country also need good methods of travel and communication in their work.

In the past our forefathers walked and sometimes carried their belongings on their heads. This method was extremely slow and tedious. Also not many things could be carried by this method of transport, called *head porterage*.

In north Ghana some animals were used for transport. The *draught animals* (horses and donkeys) were not suitable in the forest areas. This is because the tsetse fly, the insect which causes sleeping sickness, attacked them in the forests.

The old ways of travelling have greatly changed. There are now four main ways of travelling and carrying things from one place to another. These are railways (trains), roads (cars and lorries), water (ships, boats and canoes) and air (aeroplanes).

Line	Length	Period built	Purpose
1. Sekondi-Kumasi (extended to Takoradi in 1927)	170 miles (274 km)	1896–1903 (extended 1927)	(1) to serve the mining areas (Tarkwa and Obuasi) (2) to transport timber (3) to help in opening up the country
2. Accra-Kumasi	192 miles (309 km)	1909–23	(1) to serve the cocoa-growing areas (2) to transport timber, and later bauxite from the mines near Nkawkaw
3. Tarkwa-Prestea	18 miles (29 km)	1912	to serve the gold mines at Prestea
4. Huni Valley-Kade	99 miles (159 km)	1928	(1) to help in opening new areas for cocoa (2) to transport timber (3) to serve the diamond fields in the Birim Valley
5. Dunkwa-Awaso	46 miles (74 km)	1940	(1) to serve the bauxite mines at Awaso (2) to transport cocoa and timber
6. Achimota-Tema	16 miles (26 km)	1954	to help in carrying heavy equipment to Tema for harbour building
7. Tema-Shai Hills	18 miles (29 km)	1954	to transport rock for the building of Tema Harbour
8. Achiasi-Kotoku	59 miles (95 km)	1956	to help in carrying heavy equipment from Takoradi to Tema for harbour building

The major railway lines in Ghana

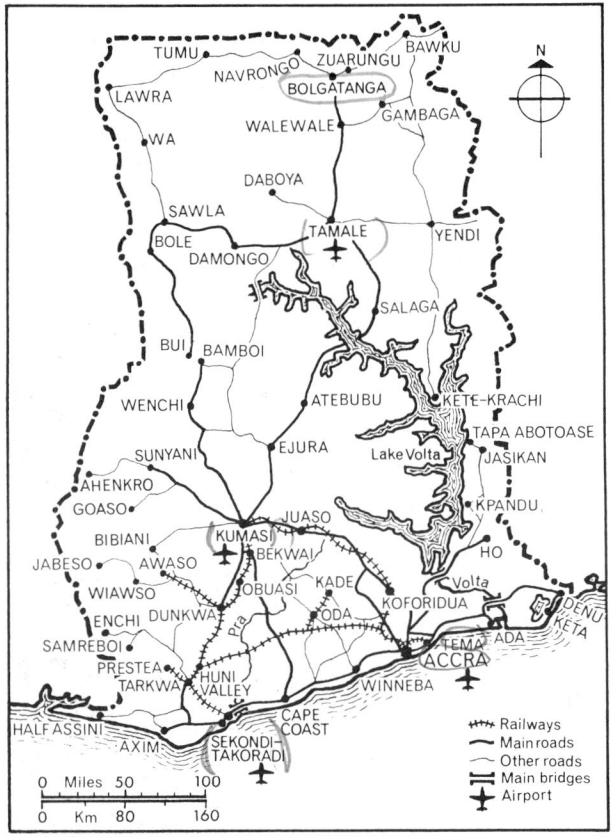

The main transport routes of Ghana

Railways

There are now 618 miles (995 km) of main railway in Ghana. The eight main railway lines are shown in the table on page 43.

People travel on trains using almost all the lines. (See the map opposite.)

In addition to the eight important lines there are several short ones, especially in the mining areas. They are used for collecting ore and for moving mining equipment from one mine to another.

The observation car of a modern diesel train

Log trains transport the sawn timber from the forest to the sawmill

Roads

You can see on the map that the total length of roads is much greater than the total length of railways. People began using cars and lorries at the beginning of the twentieth century, and roads were built to carry these vehicles. Now many parts of the country, especially south Ghana and Ashanti, are covered by roads. The existing roads are being improved, and new ones are being built to join villages to towns.

Many of the main roads of Ghana pass through Kumasi. These are Kumasi-Accra, Kumasi-Cape Coast, Kumasi-Bibiani, Kumasi-Sunyani, Kumasi-Wenchi and Kumasi-Tamale. Other roads are Tamale-Bolgatanga, Tamale-Yendi, Tamale-Lawra, Accra-Axim and Accra-Ho. There is also the Accra-Tema *motorway* on which vehicles can travel very fast.

Road transport has many uses and has helped many parts of Ghana to develop. People travel by road and carry their goods to the market for sale.

The Adomi Bridge over the Volta river

A new motorway coach, designed and built in Ghana

Coaches carry shoppers home from market

Clearing a new road through the forest

Water transport

This was important in the past, when railways and roads were not developed. As we learned in Chapter 6, some rivers were used to float timber and to carry people. Canoes are still used on some rivers and lagoons, for example Keta, by the people who live along them. Water transport is again becoming important on the Volta, where big launches carry goods from one part of the lake to another.

On the sea people travel in ships, and goods are transported to and from Ghana. We shall talk about the harbours of Ghana later.

Air transport

The most recent means of travelling is by air. But this is only possible from the four principal towns of Ghana: Accra, Kumasi, Tamale and Takoradi. Travel by air in Ghana started during the Second World War. Ghana was then served by West African Airways. Ghana Airways was formed in 1958.

Air transport is very fast, and it is used by businessmen, traders and government officials. It takes under 30 minutes to travel by air from Accra to Kumasi, about $5\frac{1}{2}$ hours faster than the express train travelling between the two towns. Ghana is linked by air routes to other parts of the world. From the Kotoka International Airport at Accra, large planes, for example the VC10, and the Boeing 707, leave for London, Rome, Cairo and many other world centres.

Exercises

1. On an outline map of the world show four countries which import cocoa from Ghana. Show their ports and draw lines to indicate the sea-route from them to Tema.

Waiting to board the ferry at Yeji, Lake Volta

Large ships carry Ghana's exports and imports

A Ghana Airways VC10

19. Takoradi and Tema Harbours

An aerial photo of Takoradi harbour

In the past there were many landing places or small ports along the coast of Ghana. Some of them are shown on the map below. The early European traders had their stations or factories in these places. Ghanaians came to some of them, which quickly grew to become important towns. Some of the towns were Axim, Shama, Sekondi, Cape Coast, Saltpond, Winneba, Accra, Prampram, Ada and Keta. These were places which had transport links with the country away from the coast. The transport links were rivers or important footpaths.

These ports were small and could not take big ships. The coast faces the Atlantic Ocean and the sea was often very rough with huge waves called *surf*. Also, the waves washed great masses of sand on to the beaches so that big ships could not come close to land. Their passengers and cargoes were carried to and from the ships by special crews in small boats. They needed great skill, as the work was often dangerous. *Piers* were built out into the water for small boats, but later these became unsuitable.

After 1918 Ghana exported and imported even greater quantities of goods. A new large port had to be built to handle this trade. The harbour at Takoradi was started in 1921 and completed in 1928. It was later extended in 1951–6 to handle more goods. Some of the goods

Loading logs in Takoradi harbour

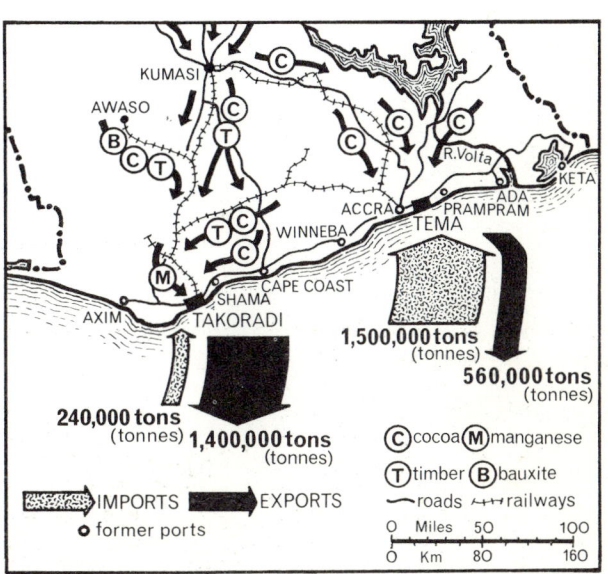

The ports of Ghana

were manganese, bauxite, timber and cocoa. Takoradi harbour helped to increase the amount of manganese, bauxite and timber produced, because it enabled producers to export them quickly.

The rapid growth of Accra and the plan to obtain electricity from the Volta made it necessary to have a second modern port. Tema was chosen as the site. It was a little fishing village, about 20 miles (32 km) east of Accra. Work to build the Tema artificial harbour began in 1952, and the harbour was opened for use in 1961. It is much bigger than Takoradi harbour. It has a *dry dock* where ships are taken out of the water to be repaired and painted. It also has a fishing harbour and a section for large oil tankers. (See the plan of Tema harbour below.)

You can see from the diagrams opposite that before 1961 Takoradi handled most of the imports and exports of Ghana. Accra received some imports but the number of exports which passed through its port was very small. The other small ports had a much smaller share of both imports and exports. Accra ceased to do the work of a port after 1962. The other small ports, for example Cape Coast, Axim and Winneba, are also no longer exporting and importing goods.

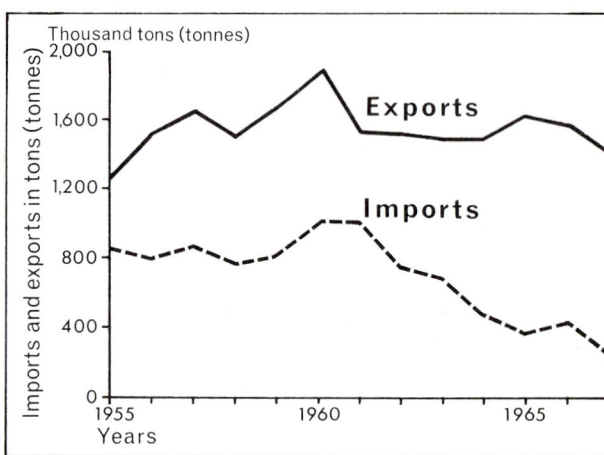

Imports and exports through Takoradi, 1955–67

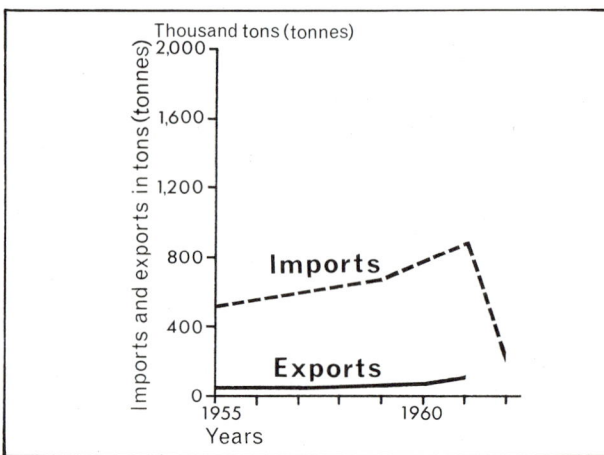

Imports and exports through Accra, 1955–62

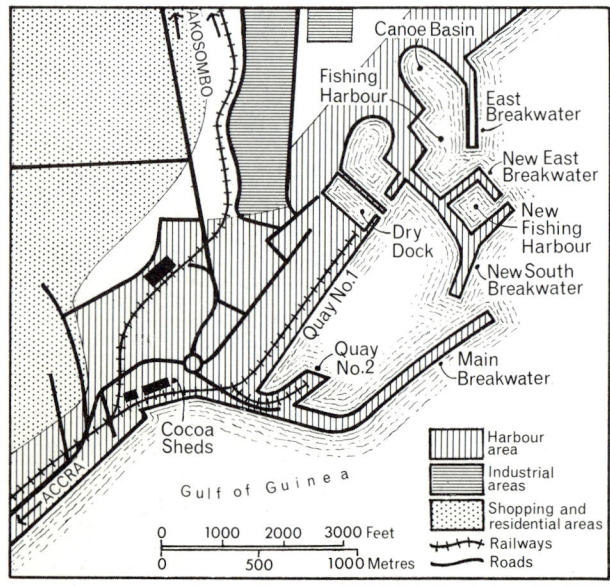

Tema harbour

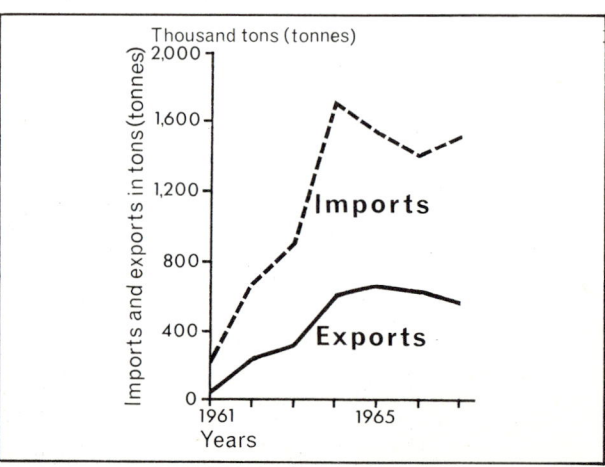

Imports and exports through Tema, 1961–7

From the diagrams you can see that Takoradi takes more of Ghana's exports than Tema. Most of the imports, however, go through Tema. Examine the diagrams; if you add together imports and exports through Takoradi, and imports and exports through Tema, you find that in 1966 Tema handled more goods than Takoradi. This has been happening since 1964.

Tema has good roads which link it to many parts of the country. From Tema you can go to Accra by a first class road or a motorway. There is a railway line which joins the main Accra-Kumasi line near Achimota. There are also good roads to Akosombo, Ho and Keta. Other important reasons why Tema is busier than Takoradi are that Tema serves a part of Ghana that has a high population, and it has more places (*berths*) for ships to anchor than Takoradi.

Exercises

1. The *hinterland* is the part of a country round a port which is served by that port. Compare the activities in the hinterlands of Takoradi and Tema.
2. Name two other artificial harbours in West Africa, besides Takoradi and Tema.
3. Name one natural harbour in West Africa.
4. What is the difference between a natural harbour and an artificial harbour?

A ship being loaded in Tema harbour

20. External Trade

All countries trade. They export some of their products to other countries, and import from other parts of the world those things which they are unable to produce themselves. This type of trade is known as *external trade*. It can also be called *international trade* because it is between nations. It is different from *internal trade* which takes place inside countries between different towns and villages. The main *commodities* or trading items of internal trade are foodstuffs, craft products etc.

We have mentioned that Ghana trades with other countries. Let us look at Ghana's external trade more closely. In 1970 Ghana received about ₵470 million from the products exported to other parts of the world. In return she imported or bought, in the same year, goods which were valued at about ₵420 million. Ghana's main exports are cocoa, timber, minerals (gold, manganese, diamonds and bauxite) and certain manufactured goods, for example bags, shoes and aluminium products. The main imports are building materials, machinery, lorries and cars, food and drink, books and stationery, and clothing.

Below is a table showing Ghana's *trading partners* (the countries to whom she sent exports or from whom she received imports) in 1970. It shows how much Ghana bought from them and how much they bought from Ghana.

These figures show two important points. First, the amount of trade with countries in the temperate regions (see Chapter 1) is much greater than with African countries. Second, Ghana imports more goods from other parts of Africa than they buy from her.

Exercises

1. Why do you think the amount of trade between Ghana and countries in temperate regions is greater than trade between Ghana and other African countries? Look back to page 2.
2. Why does Ghana import more goods from other parts of Africa than they buy from her?

Country or area	Imports (million ₵)	Exports (million ₵)
United Kingdom	99·1	109·4
Western Europe (West Germany, Netherlands, Italy, France, etc.)	91·5	112·3
USA and Canada	80·3	89·3
USSR, Eastern Europe and China	34·6	74·3
Japan	25·8	30·3
African countries	21·7	4·2
Others (Australia, New Zealand, India, etc.)	66·0	47·5
	419·0	**467·3**

Ghana's trading partners

Sacks of cocoa for export being loaded at Tema harbour

USA

The American pavilion at an international trade fair in Accra

51

21. The People of Ghana and Where they Live

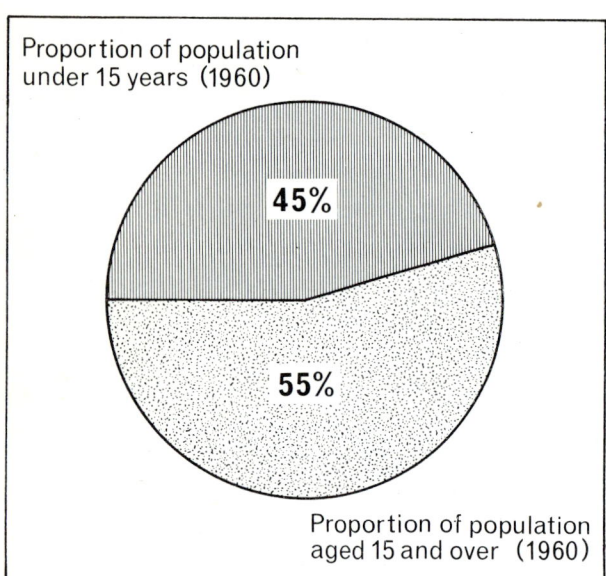

Proportion of population under 15 years (1960)

45%

55%

Proportion of population aged 15 and over (1960)

Age distribution in Ghana

Ghana's population has been increasing steadily. As you can see from the population graph below, the population increased from 3·5 million in 1931 to 4·1 million in 1948, 6·7 million in 1960 and 8·5 million in 1970. The population of the country has grown by about 143 per cent since 1931. This means that for every 100 people in 1931 there are now 243 people. The population is therefore nearly two and a half times the size it was in 1931.

The main reason for the increase in the Ghanaian population is the improvement in health services. There are now more hospitals, health centres, clinics and maternity homes than in the past. Not many babies die at birth or soon afterwards, and people now live longer.

From the diagram opposite you can see that in 1960 children under the age of 15 formed a large part of the population. The problem of getting

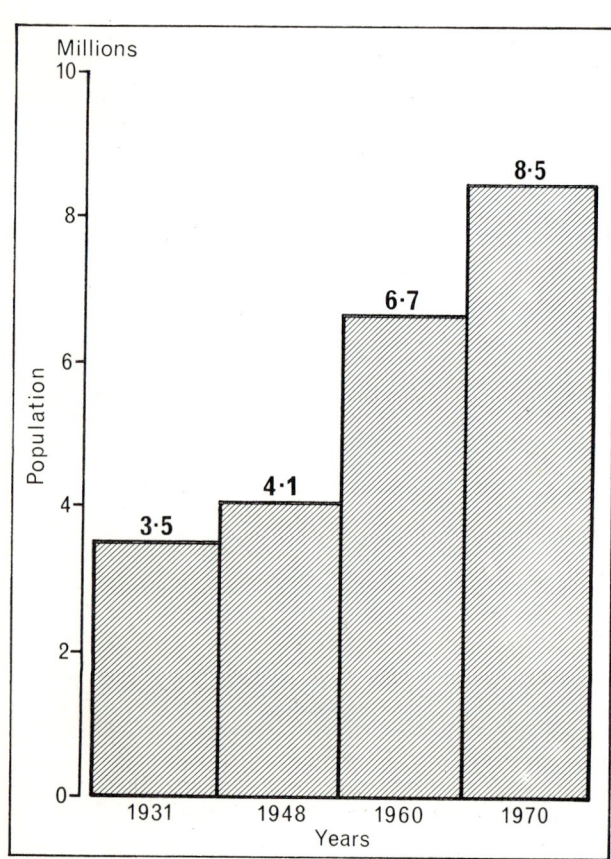

Population graph, 1931–70

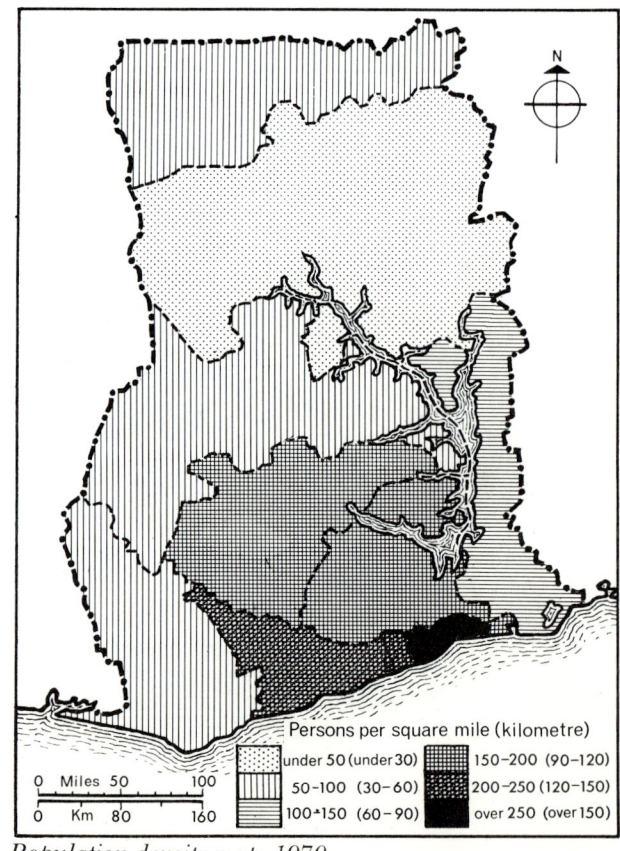

Population density map, 1970

work for some of them who have now grown up had become difficult. When the children leave school they increase the working population.

In 1960 there were about 73 persons per square mile in Ghana (45 persons per sq. km). Now this figure has increased to 93 persons per square mile (58 persons per sq. km). What this means is that if the people of Ghana were spread evenly over the country there would be 93 persons in each area measuring one mile by one mile (or 58 persons in each area measuring one kilometre by one kilometre).

But not every square mile (kilometre) of land has exactly the same number of people. (See the population density map opposite.) Some parts have more people than others. The number (*density*) of the population is high in the Greater Accra, Central Eastern and Ashanti Regions. It is low in the Northern, Brong Ahafo and Upper Regions. People are attracted by work. So the population is high in the areas where there are chances for employment. There are more people in the southern part of the country than in the north. In the south are most of the big towns and the cocoa-growing areas.

The areas with less than 93 persons per square mile (58 persons per sq. km) are mostly in places where the rainfall is generally low. Crops such as cocoa and coffee cannot be grown in these places. People have left these areas for the south. Some diseases, for example river blindness along the Red Volta, force the inhabitants in these areas to *migrate*, or move, to other places.

Exercises
1. Look again at the population density map. Which region has the highest density of population? Give three reasons to explain this.
2. Which region has the lowest density of population? Give three reasons to explain this.

A village settlement in the country. Notice how the houses are grouped in a circle with space between them

New housing at Tema. Here the buildings are closer together. They are in rows and there is no centre

22. The Towns of Ghana

Liberty Avenue, Accra

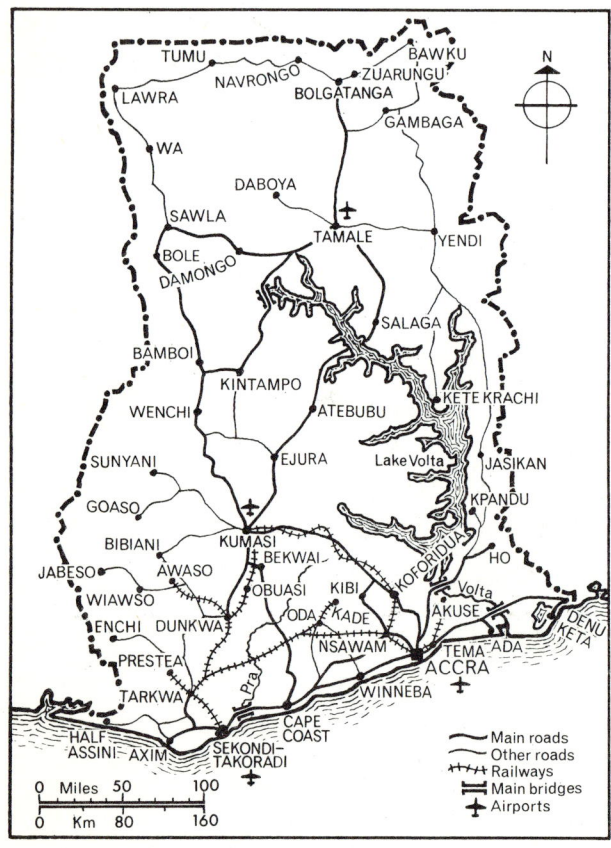

The towns of Ghana

Ghana has more than 100 towns with over 5,000 inhabitants each. A few of these are really large with over 50,000 people each. But the size of the population should not be the only thing to look for when we want to know the important towns of Ghana.

Towns must have many workers, just a few of whom should be farmers. The rest work in factories, offices, banks, stores and in the market. Towns may also be *centres of administration* which means that they have men whose job it is to look after public affairs and services, both in the town and in the land around it. Many have schools, colleges, hospitals, cinemas and other services.

The important towns of Ghana have been located on the map opposite. You can see that they are all important centres of transport. Some of those along the coast have railways, roads and harbours. In the centre of south Ghana is Kumasi, where many roads and the two main railway lines meet.

The important towns are growing faster than the less important ones and the villages. Many people are moving, or migrating, from the villages (*rural areas*) to the towns. The population of Accra increased from 140,000 in 1948 to 350,000 in 1960. It has been growing very

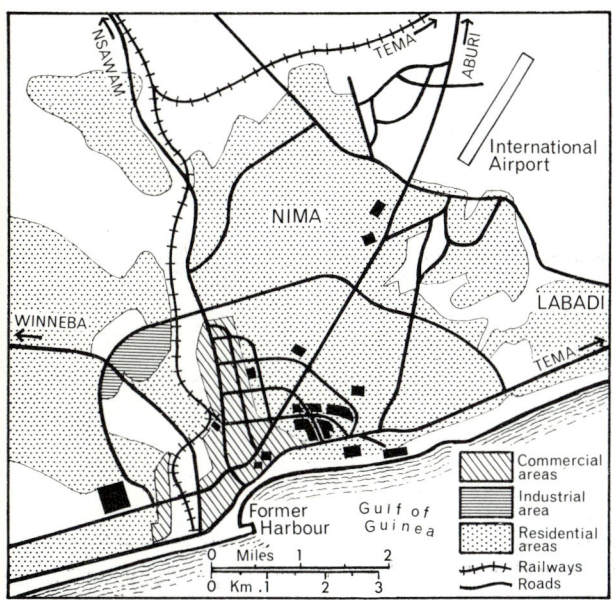

A plan of Accra

Kingsway Stores in Accra

rapidly in recent years. As young boys and girls finish school, a great many of them go to Accra and Tema to find jobs in factories, stores and offices.

We can divide the important towns of Ghana into three groups:
(1) harbours and industrial towns, e.g. Takoradi and Tema. *Industrial* towns are those with factories, where goods are manufactured.
(2) mining and commercial towns, e.g. Obuasi and Tarkwa. *Commercial* towns are those which handle business and trade.
(3) adminstrative, commercial and industrial towns, e.g. Accra and Kumasi. *Administrative* towns are those which control public affairs.

Tamale, Bolgatanga, Koforidua, Cape Coast, Ho and Sunyani belong to group (3), but we have to remember that they do not have many modern industries.

Every town has something which makes it important. Some towns are important for several things. Cape Coast is an administrative and commercial centre. What is the other activity of this town which makes it well known?

For a town to develop properly its inhabitants must feel that they belong to it. Many of the main towns have important chiefs. They are ruled by *councils*, which are groups of people whose members are *elected* or chosen by the people themselves.

Accra

Accra has a population of over 600,000. It is the capital of Ghana. It is built on low hills separated by valleys, some of which are flooded in the rainy season.

Accra was a small village until the middle of the seventeenth century when Ussher Fort and James Fort were built. Accra became a trading post. It started to grow much faster after 1877 when it became the capital of Ghana, instead of Cape Coast which was the former capital.

Accra became a very active port from 1900 onwards when the country began to export cocoa in large quantities. Accra's function as the main port, commercial centre and capital of Ghana became more important when it was linked to the rest of the country by railways and roads. Accra is no longer a port. But it is still very busy as the capital and commercial centre. It has many industries, the Kotoka International Airport and the University of Ghana. Some of Accra's main buildings are shown on page 56.

The Central Library, Accra

Kotoka International Airport

The University of Ghana at Legon

The Law Courts, Accra

The University of Science and Technology at Kumasi

Kumasi

Kumasi is the second largest town in Ghana.
It has a population of about 350,000. It was
called Kwaman when Oti Akenten and his
followers occupied it about 400 years ago, and has
since been the capital of Ashanti. It was destroyed
three times by the British, in 1874, 1896 and 1901.

The factors which helped it to grow rapidly
were (1) modern transport (railways and roads),
(2) trade and commerce, (3) being made the centre
of administration by the British, and
(4) industrialization and education.

Kumasi is the meeting place of the two main
railway lines in Ghana. It is also the point where
five main roads meet. It now has many stores
and its central market is one of the busiest in
Ghana. As the capital of the Ashanti Region,
Kumasi has many government departments with
a large number of *civil servants*. These are people
who do the work of the Government. Since
1950 a number of industries have developed.
Some of these are sawmills, a jute factory, a
shoe factory and breweries. It has the University
of Science and Technology and the Ghana
National Cultural Centre. It is also the seat of
the Asantehene.

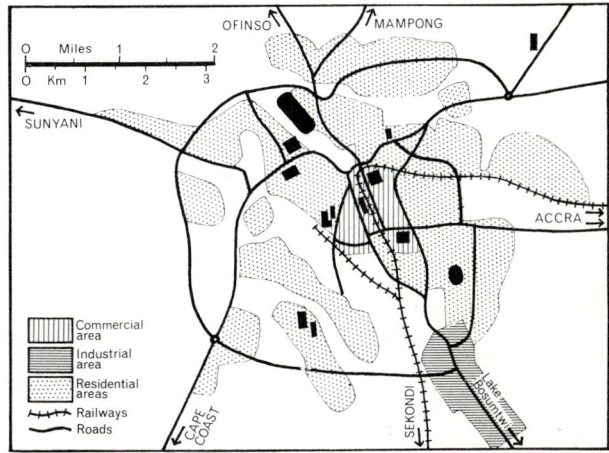

A plan of Kumasi

Exercises

1. Name any town you know. Draw a sketch map
to show its position in Ghana. Make a list of the
activities which go on in the town. Show on
the map the villages which the town serves.
2. Draw a sketch plan of any other town you
know. Show on the plan the market and shopping
area. Show where the people live and other
buildings in the town, e.g. schools and colleges.

57

23. Villages in the Forest Areas

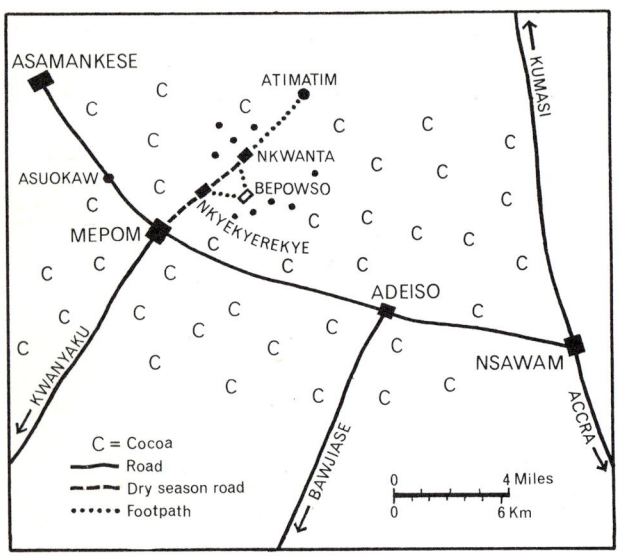

A plan of the Nkwanta area

About three out of every four Ghanaians live in villages. Some villages are large and have certain activities usually seen in towns. Such villages may have colleges, hospitals and stores. Others are small with only a few houses.

Many of the villages in Ghana are in the forest areas. The *inhabitants* (the people who live in the villages) are mainly farmers. They grow cocoa, coffee, tobacco and food crops. Some of them may be craftsmen making baskets, cutlasses, chairs and stools.

Let us look at some villages. On the busy road between Nsawam and Asamantese is Mepom. It is a large village with a post office, market, stores and fitters' shops. This is a central village with a number of small ones around it. One of the small villages is Nkwanta, about four miles (6 km) north-east of Mepom. (See the diagram opposite.)

A village in the forest area

The inhabitants of Nkwanta and most of the hamlets around it are farmers who have migrated from Akwapim. Nkwanta has a church and a school, for the farmers and their children. It is a busy place from October to January when cocoa is harvested and sold.

One of the hamlets around Nkwanta is Bepowso. (Look for it on the diagram.) It has four compounds. Each is on the land of its owner. Opanyin Kwame, one of the farmers, leads a simple but interesting life.

In January and February he makes new farms in which he grows yams, maize, cocoyams and cocoa. In May and June he weeds his cocoa farms. From October to December he plucks his cocoa, dries the beans and sells them. He is helped by his wife and grandchildren. The children go to school at Nkwanta.

Opanyin Kwame's house is simple. It consists of six bedrooms, a patio and a kitchen. The compound is fenced. Opanyin Kwame keeps sheep and goats inside the fence. He sells them from time to time. In the compound are two raised platforms for drying cocoa beans.

Exercises
1. Draw a sketch map of the area in which your school is located. Show on the map four villages or towns which are in the area.
2. Make a list of all the activities which take place in one of the villages or towns. Why do you say it is a village or a town? What is the difference between them?

The compound of a house like Opanyin Kwame's

Preparing the evening meal

24. Villages in the North

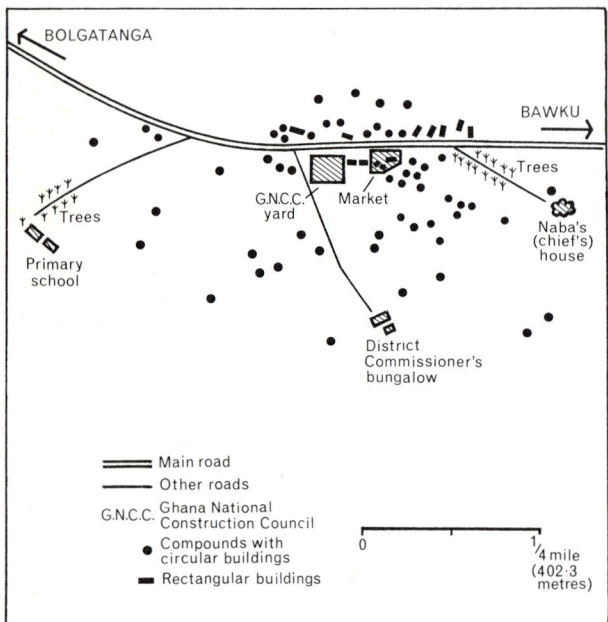

A plan of Nangodi

Map legend:
- ═══ Main road
- ——— Other roads
- G.N.C.C. Ghana National Construction Council
- • Compounds with circular buildings
- ▬ Rectangular buildings

0   ¼ mile (402·3 metres)

Map labels: BOLGATANGA, BAWKU, Trees, G.N.C.C. yard, Market, Trees, Naba's (chief's) house, Primary school, District Commissioner's bungalow

You now know something about the work done in villages in the forest areas of Ghana. You can also describe the form of some of them. Villages in the northern savannah are, in some ways, like those in the forest areas. The chief occupation is farming. There are also some craftsmen. Among these may be basket weavers, tailors making smocks, and people making leather goods. Two other activities which may also be found are the making of shea butter, and the brewing of *pito*, a drink made from millet and guinea corn.

In the northern savannah, some villages are *nucleated*, that is their houses are grouped together. Others are *dispersed*, that is they have scattered compounds or houses.

Nangodi is one of these dispersed villages. It is located on the Bolgatanga-Bawku road. (See the diagram opposite.) It has a school. If we visit this place in September or October we shall see that there are a few compounds along the road. In the centre of them is a market which attracts many sellers and buyers on market days. At this time of the year a large part of the village will be hidden by millet and guinea corn growing in the fields. Most of the scattered houses become visible in the dry season.

Each compound is surrounded by the owner's farmlands. The farmer tries to keep the land fertile by putting manure such as cow dung on to the soil.

The plan of the compounds is different from that seen in the south, and in the large towns of north Ghana. The compounds are circular with a number of rooms which are also circular. Some of the rooms have roofs made of thatch, others are made of mud. Grain (millet and guinea corn) is dried on the mud roofs. People can also rest on them, especially on warm evenings.

In Nangodi we shall find that the rooms of the compounds are used in different ways. Many are bedrooms. Some are used as kitchens, *granaries* (where grain is kept) and as pens for sheep.

Exercises
1. What is the difference between a nucleated village and a dispersed village?
2. What are some of the differences between villages in the south and in the north of Ghana?

Entering the central room of the compound

A compound in north Ghana

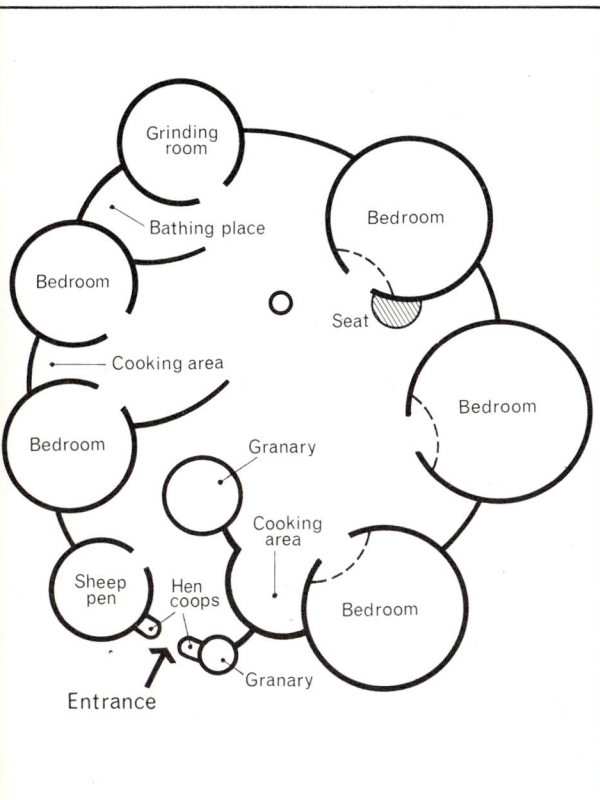

Grinding room

Bathing place

Bedroom

Bedroom

Seat

Cooking area

Bedroom

Bedroom

Granary

Cooking area

Sheep pen

Hen coops

Bedroom

Entrance

Granary

Plan of a compound in Nangodi

Thatched granaries, built on sticks for protection